The Pursuit of His Calling: Following in Purpose

The Pursuit of His Calling: Following in Purpose

Dr. Florence Muindi

THE PURSUIT OF HIS CALLING: FOLLOWING IN PURPOSE

Copyright © 2008 Florence N. Muindi

Published by:

Integrity Publishers Inc.
P.O. Box 798,
Wakeforest, NC 27588
USA.
info@integritypublishers.org

ISBN 13: 978-0-9821175-0-7

ISBN 10: 0-9821175-0-7

All Scripture quotations, unless otherwise indicated, are from the Holy Bible, New International Version®. NIV®. Copyright © 1973, 1978, 1984, by International Bible Society. Used by permission of Zondervan Publishing House. All rights reserved.

The proceeds of the purchase of this book goes towards supporting the Ministry of Life in Abundance International.

Printed in India by Thomson Press

Dedication

This book is dedicated to:

All who serve with Life in Abundance Ministry.

May you always be reminded of the humble beginning of this ministry.

The reader:

May this cause you to applaud God,

who is faithful and good in all He does.

Acknowledgements

I am indebted to both my nuclear and extended family. They have allowed me to share stories that render them vulnerable. I'm deeply thankful, especially to my husband Festus and our boys, Jay and Kyalo. Thank you for bearing so much with me.

Cathy Baldizon was the first to encourage me to share this testimony, and she took the time to edit the first draft. Thank you Cathy for being a dear friend and coach.

This testimony would not be possible without each and every partner who has helped in this work in one way or the other. Our fellow CMF missionaries, prayer and financial supporters, the national churches, accountability partners, LIA staff, and past and present colleagues, among others. I am truly thankful that together God's kingdom has come in the way He wanted us to further it.

I am very thankful to a friend who recently went to be with the Lord: LIA board member, Dr Berhanu Habte. He dearly supported us, shared his wisdom, and modeled the life of a true disciple, especially at a time when the ministry work was just beginning in Ethiopia.

Finally to Dad who was my hero. He taught me to stop at nothing and pointed beyond the limits for me. A great life direction was set in motion by him, and he is a best friend ever. Thank you, 'Nau', for loving me so.

Contents

Foreword

CMF takes a careful evaluation of our recruits to assess their preparation for cross-cultural missions. The CMF home office, our field teams, boards and other avenues are utilized in the exercise. Interviews then follow and a short-term assignment sometimes helps clarify if short-term missionaries will develop into career missionaries. The Muindis were in a special class, coming from Africa yet called to serve Africa. They were among our first three of such families. Their focus was to serve in Ethiopia.

The last quarter of a century has seen remarkable hardship visited upon the people of Ethiopia. Famines and wars of attrition have led to tremendous loss of life, rampant poverty, devastation of farmland and destruction of infrastructure. Basic human needs—clean water, health care, simple nutrition, and employment—have gone unmet. Added to this has been the AIDS pandemic.

When Dr. Florence Muindi and her family moved to Addis Ababa, God led them to embark upon a ministry of transformational development among the poor. They came prepared, having backgrounds in medicine and business administration, and serving previously as missionaries among the pastoral Maasai people of Kenya.

The majority of the world's Christians now live in the southern hemisphere. The Christian center of gravity has moved from West to East and from North to South. Missionaries are sent from many countries. Festus and Florence Muindi are representative of this new breed of missionary. You will thrill with what they have been able to accomplish in such a desperate situation. Their ministry--incarnational, innovative, and effective--brings glory to God.

Doug Priest
Executive Director
CMF International

Introduction

"In that day you will say: Give thanks to the Lord, call on His name; make known among the nations what He has done, and proclaim that His name is exalted. Sing to the Lord, for He has done glorious things; let this be known to all the world"
(Isaiah 12: 4-5).

Most of what is written in this book comes from my journaling. This is a practice I have kept since my teen years. At the end of each day, I pause to put down my experiences. Raw thoughts, frustrations, joys, feelings, all get recorded on my journal pages. As I write, then review later, I get to process and learn how God is leading. This has characterized my life. Both the high moments on the "mountains" as well as very low ones in the valleys of life have become, altogether, a sweet flavour in pursuit of God, who has called me and remains faithful.

This is another milestone in my life. As I expose my journaling, I feel I am taking a risk, laying bare what would be best securely tucked away until I am gone. It makes me feel naked, exposed, and therefore vulnerable. But if in so doing this story serves to encourage another Christian pilgrim, then the risk is worthwhile.

The Holy Spirit has compelled me to tell this story. This brings back to memory two people who have helped me overcome what could have been moments of procrastination. One of those was Muthoki, my dear friend in third grade who helped me in knowing Christ as Lord and Saviour. The other is Dr. Berhanu Habte who recently went to be with the Lord. He was a very dear servant of God and founding member of the LIA International board. Dr. Berhanu urged us to always act, if compelled by the Holy Spirit, even when it costs. As was the case with Paul, potential adversities did not hinder his task of preaching the gospel of God's grace.

And so I take courage to tell my story of God's leading so far. God has instructed, taught, counseled and watched over me for the glory of His name. I testify to the sufficiency of His leading in everyday life. I pray that my story will contribute to the cause of the gospel by adding impetus to the expansion of our Lord's kingdom.

Florence Muindi's Journal:
October 4th, 2008.

Chapter 1

The Covenant

It was the final week of high school, and I was scared. I feared leaving the guided life at school. The world out there with its many hard choices was scary. How would I know which ones were right? What if I ended up in the wrong career? What if I ended up being miserable, with irreversible consequences? How do people have the courage to live with such uncertainty in issues of life?

What had started as an ordinary evening led to serious and deep searching as my thoughts relentlessly focused on questions about life's purpose. I remembered very clearly what had happened five months earlier. I had not really fully processed the event at the time and it had lingered, half-baked and tucked in the back of my mind, as I dealt with the pressure of exams and school projects. Suddenly, what had transpired came back into my mind. And what an event it was!

It had begun as an interruption in my chemistry class. Chemistry, Mathematics, and Biology were the subjects I was taking for the Advanced Level curriculum. Growing up in Kenya in the first three decades post-independence meant a British curriculum in the country's schools. It included seven years of primary school, then four years of ordinary level high school, followed by two years of advanced level before university entry. I was in that last year of advanced level.

In the midst of a chemistry experiment, I was told that the Principal, a Mrs. Karanja, wanted to see me immediately. I quickly cleaned up my desktop and left for the famous office.

Why famous? You had to have done something extremely serious to be summoned there. The two-minute walk had my mind guessing what it could be. I imagined that as a dormitory prefect, it could be that I needed to explain something pertaining to my responsibility.

However, when I saw my stepbrother James and a brother-in-law in the headmistress' waiting room, I knew something more serious had happened. I became even more disturbed when they avoided eye contact with me. Instead, they quickly let me know the head teacher was waiting for me, and I needed to go straight in.

Our time with the head teacher was brief. Coming out of her office, I was even more confused. All she told me was that my relatives had come to pick me up to go home to attend to an event there. As a result, I needed to go pack a few basic items and join them. She then accompanied me to the outer office to make sure I obeyed the instructions without attempting to get more information from my relatives.

All this time, I was left to imagine the worst. I knew that the only thing that could have me going home in the middle of a school week would be the death of a close relative. I prayed that it would not be my Dad. Anyone else, but not him.

Dad had been my source of support and encouragement, especially at that particular time. He had convinced me to aim high in my academic pursuit, promising to be there to help me. He was my cheerleader. When it came to making decisions, his word of advice was the best. No, I couldn't do without him.

Dad and I had a unique relationship. We would stay up late to talk, and we spent quality time "dreaming" together. This was the case in spite of Dad having twenty of us! I was the third child of his second wife. My mother had ten children, and my stepmother had ten also. I knew God would hear my prayer and answer it, so I prayed that it would not be Dad, and then I felt a special peace – an assurance that God was in charge and that I needed not worry. By the time I joined my two relatives for the ride home, I was well composed and without any questions. Sensing this, they found no immediate need to explain the reason for their coming for me.

Meanwhile, we began to chat about my school and farming activities along the road until they sort of forgot I needed to know why I was going home. Then, as though suddenly remembering something, my stepbrother pulled over to the roadside, turned to face me in the back seat and announced that they needed to explain what had happened. In response, I took a deep breath and I assured him I was ready to hear because I had prayed about it and I knew God had heard me. In a solemn voice, he made the announcement. Dad had died. He had died suddenly in a road accident by our gate at home. I was too overcome to follow the rest of the details.

Immediately I turned to God. How could He not have prevented this? I thought the promises made between Dad and I were known to God. Just how was I supposed to make it in life without Dad? What about all my younger sisters and brothers? Dad was our breadwinner. God had surely gotten it all wrong! How was life going to be without my cheerleader? Was there even any reason to go back to school? Then I suddenly remembered I had prayed and I knew God had heard me! So, I decided I was not going to cry. I was going to look to God and agree with Him. His way was still best.

And we know that in all things God works for the good of those who love Him, who have been called according to His purpose.
— *Romans 8:28*

I made an effort to regain composure, faced the bearer of the bad news and nodded to make him know that I understood what he had said. He asked me if I had any questions to ask and I shook my head to show that I had none. He then turned around, started the car, and we drove home.

What followed was a very sad and difficult week. By the time I got home, my mother had cried herself hoarse. Her red swollen eyes told it all. My sisters and brothers were equally distraught. But to everyones' surprise, I remained calm and did not talk much or cry. I had decided I was not going to cry. I was going to accept what had happened without complaining. God loved me, He knew it all before it happened, yet He permitted it.

But I must admit I also didn't sleep much that week. I thought much about the life that had just passed on. Dad had been an only child. His father was killed in the First World War, where he had forcibly been enrolled as a porter. That was my grandfather. His friends who survived the war brought back his snuffbox and blanket. This was a confirmation to my grandmother that her husband was no more.

My grandmother grieved over this for a long time. She had been sickly and this incident compounded her weakness. One morning, she woke up and struggled to the door to let the chicken out, but at the doorpost, she collapsed and died. My dad, then three years old, was still breastfeeding. He followed her to the door and, finding her lying down, lay by her to breastfeed. He was found hours later by the neighbors still sucking at his dead mother's breast.

Now that his parents were both dead, a distant relative who was a widow with no children took in Dad. She brought Dad up and took good care of him.

As a teenager in the then Kenya colony, Dad was volunteered by the clan to be the one to attend the then British Government schools. Each family was supposed to give one boy to be enrolled in school, but my father's relatives' aim in volunteering him was to take away his land which he was supposed to inherit..

In school, Dad proved to be a very gifted student. He did well in his exams, getting a leather belt as an award from the school principal for making it to the highest level and for graduating to join a teacher training college. Thus, he became a pioneer teacher in our district and was instrumental in starting up the Anglican Church in the area.

Upon getting his job as a teacher, he bought a few cows and managed to marry his first wife, my stepmother, and together they had eight children. Then he married my mother and went on to have another two more children with my stepmother and ten of us with my mother.

In total, he brought up twenty of us and his youngest child was three when he died.

He did, however, get into some trouble for marrying Mom as a second wife. He was relieved of his duties as a church leader and put on discipline. He was also prohibited from participating in the Lord's Supper. Nevertheless, he continued to attend the same church up to the time of his death.

At the home level, Dad brought us up in a Christian manner. He would lead us in devotions every evening and he would pray for each of us before we went to bed. He taught us the Word of God and corrected us using it. I had grown to love my Dad and greatly admired him. We had become the best of friends.

Two days after his funeral, I took a bus and went back to school. End of term exams were drawing near and I needed to put behind what had happened and move on.

Three days after returning to school, and in the middle of a mathematics class, the reality of the loss of my father hit me. It came very suddenly. I was working on solving a problem and the struggle to find the answer reminded me of my situation. Dad was gone and I was on my own. Alone! I was going to have to struggle to make it in life without him, with no cheerleader to encourage me. And even if I were to make it, he would not be there to celebrate with me. I do not recall the details of what followed but I must have screamed and thrown my books down. I was stopped as I ran towards the door. I cried hysterically for hours. Then I was hospitalized for four days and remained on medication for two weeks.

Over time, I pulled through the grief and again got busy with my school work. Unfortunately, I had shelved that event without processing it. But now, on this November evening, five months later, as I prepared to graduate and leave advanced level school, the fear of what the future held for me brought the death of my father to focus again.

I wondered what life for me would be like without Dad. Would I get to be friends with my mother? How about guidance and companionship? If anything, this was the time I needed guidance most, especially as I considered college, a career, and even marriage at a later date.

Then I sought to understand the real meaning of life. Why live just to die? What does it all mean? If I die poor or rich, successful or a failure, what difference does it make? I might enjoy life, but so what? What is life's purpose?

Then I asked myself, do I have a purpose in life? I remembered I wanted to please Dad. I wanted to be approved of him and make him proud. And I had. I worked hard in my primary school for him and, sure enough, he appreciated it. I scored very well in all the national exams. By merit, I had been admitted to what was then the best schools in the country, ending up in the same dormitory with the then President's daughter. My performance brought Dad much joy. It was an affirmation of a successful school principal, whose children modeled exemplary students.

My dad had impacted so many things in my life. After the four years of high school, I found out that Dad spoke highly of a different high school. This school excelled in sciences and Dad thought I was good at them. So I chose that school for my advanced level education. Sure enough, with Dad as my cheerleader, I was the first of only two girls to be admitted there from my first high school. That gave me a very high chance of being admitted to a government university on full scholarship. I wanted to study medicine and my Cheerleader thought it would be great; so I chose it. Without doubt, I had lived to please Dad.

On that November night, I revisited all these steps and stages in my life. What do I live for now? I got down on my knees and started talking to God. I cried more than I prayed. I asked Him to reveal His purpose for my life. To know it so I could pursue it. Four hours later, when I reached for that diary, I had come to a conclusion.

God was going to be my Hero. I would fashion my life after Christ.

I was going to give all of me to Him. I was going to live my life to bring Him glory. All that I was and ever would be was being handed over to Him, to use me as He would, for whatever He chose. Until my last breath, I was going to serve Him and Him alone. I was going to work fervently to that end, aiming for excellence.

Then I let God know that He was to help me do this. I had undertaken to live for Him, and I depended on Him for divine enablement. I asked Him to watch over me. At every turn along the way, I needed Him to accompany me. Walking hand in hand with Him was going to be the style. He had my full permission to correct me. He had my full consent to interfere with my plans. I yielded myself fully to His control. If I ever left that and refused to heed His correction, He had my permission to take my life. This was my expressed desire: it was better to depart to glory than to serve self or any other.

I will instruct you and teach you in the way you should go; I will counsel you and watch over you.

— *Psalms 32:8*

Taking a pen, I entered the date in my diary — November 19, 1981, two o'clock in the morning. With tears running down my cheeks uncontrollably, I held my pen tight, as if fearing someone might try to pull it out of my hands. But I could sense a powerful "self", not willing to let go. This was the day and the hour. It was a time of full surrender! I yielded my rights to God, allowing Him to own me. I put an end to my kingdom and surrendered to His kingdom. I wrote my pledge to Him down and signed so I wouldn't forget. I sealed the covenant with my very life by telling God to let me die if I changed my mind.

The next day, I called my elder sister, who was then married, and asked if I could meet her on Saturday to discuss something very important. She came with her husband. We later walked off in the park, just the two of us, leaving her husband sitting somewhere on a bench. I explained to my sister that I had committed my life totally to God. I had set myself apart to serve Him. I was going to be a missionary!

The women missionaries I knew from Africa were Catholic nuns. So I told her that most likely I would be becoming one. She did not have much to say. But she did tell me it was possible to serve God without becoming a nun. This was repeated to me by several people. Before long, it was clear to me that God was setting me apart, calling me to the ministry, to Himself, not to a status in society.

> *You did not choose me, but I chose you and appointed you to go and bear fruit – fruit that will last.*
>
> *— John 15:16 (a)*

Chapter 2

Small Beginnings

My stepbrother Jonah and I went to kindergarten together. Every morning, I would stop by their house across the road and we would walk to school together. Then we would walk back home together after school, getting home in time for lunch. Most afternoons were spent playing together, taking care of cows or watching over my little sister and brother. Jonah was the last-born child of my stepmother.

That kindergarten year ended fast and it was time to join grade one. We were excited. It meant we would have new school uniforms and we would be going to school in the opposite direction, where our bigger brothers and sisters went. What a great promotion!

This excitement was, however, cut short by a new development. Dad came home and announced some change. After working on his budget, he had realized that he could only afford the school uniform and registration fees for one of us. Jonah would join grade One first, and I had to wait at home until the following year.

When I eventually got to elementary school, I was eager to catch up with Jonah. I was keen to learn the basics. I unconsciously got into competition with him, and in the evenings I would work to catch up with him. This competitive approach kept me motivated and doing well in my studies.

At that time, we became friends with Muthoki, the daughter of my father's friend. We would play together and share experiences. We would also share our lunch.

One day at recess in the second term of third grade, Muthoki told me there was something she wanted to share with me. We went to a quiet corner of the school field and, she slowly and confidently, explained that over the weekend, something had happened to her life. She had invited Jesus into her heart. She then explained the basics of being born again. This made good sense and I wanted it. She then prayed with me, and I invited Jesus into my life.

One of the things she made clear to me was that I was to confess Jesus Christ before others, testifying to what He had done. Immediately we were back in class after recess, I went in front of the class and asked for their attention to speak. I confessed Christ as the Lord of my life and for reasons I do not fully recall, began to cry. This incident led to five other classmates making a commitment to Christ.

The encounter with Jesus Christ gave me a new outlook to life. I realized the meaning of what Paul says in his letter to the Galatians:

"I have been crucified with Christ and I no longer live but Christ lives in me. The life I live in the body, I live by faith in the Son of God, who loved me and gave Himself for me."
— *Galatians 2:20*

Immediately, that change began to manifest in my life. On our way to the river where we drew our water, we passed by a rather poor neighbor's house. Since the encounter with Christ, I noticed for the first time how poor this family was. I began to see people who were in need and developed the desire to help them, a reaction that was formerly not part of me. Christ began to control my life and make me aware of the needs of others.

The second term of third grade was a revival time in school. Prayer meetings would be held at recess and lunchtime. Praise sessions were common after school. The Spirit of God was moving among the student population. I know several people from that locality who made a decision for Christ at that time who continue to be strong in the Lord. Indeed, some are even involved in the Christian ministry at different levels today.

I approached my church, requesting to be baptized. As an Anglican I should have been baptized as a child, but this was not possible for me due to the family situation. My mother had been brought up in a Christian family and my grandfather was a pastor, but Mom fell in love with her teacher, who was a married man, and ran away from home to marry him. As children born out of such a relationship, we were not to be baptized.

However, following my commitment to Christ, I was allowed to enroll for the baptismal classes. After about a year of attending these classes on Saturday mornings, I was evaluated by the elders and accepted for baptism, a public declaration of my faith. My Auntie Tabitha became my godmother and I took the name Florence, signifying a new beginning in Christ. The name I received at birth, Ndinda, which means one who tarries, became my middle name.

I was very much determined to live out my faith. I began to co-lead the Sunday School class and serve in various roles in the youth ministry. My determination to be a good student and a childlike desire to please God caught the attention of my fifth grade teacher. As a result, he favoured me above the other students and this aroused jealousy among those he did not give the same treatment. My cousin happened to be one of them. She was in the same class with me, although four years older.

One particular day turned out badly for me. I had gotten into trouble for not bringing some items to school that we had been told to bring. Although the others who had also forgotten to bring what was needed were punished, I was let to go free. My classmates were unhappy and I was branded the 'teacher's pet'.

On our way home, they started to tease me, with my cousin leading them. They pushed and roughed me up calling me names all the way to our gate. When I got home, I told my mother what had transpired, crying as I narrated the story. She promised to talk to my auntie about my cousin's behavior, but I think she never did to avoid confrontation. That was just mom.

By the time I was in seventh grade, I was very committed to my schoolwork. With two other girls, I began to pursue excellence in all I did. I would stay up past midnight to study. God drew me to love my schoolwork and caused me to succeed. My two friends and I did very well and were among the best in the district. We were all admitted to a very prestigious high school.

Financially, it was a big sacrifice for Dad to put me through this boarding high school. My elder sister Ruth, who was by then working, helped pay my tuition fees. The facilities, uniform and food were excellent. Being able to get a place in that high school took God's intervention. This was a school in the city. It was the first time for me to visit Nairobi, the capital of Kenya. I was exposed to social and educational values I could never have imagined possible. God had actually opened for me a door of opportunity to receive the best education that my country could offer. Coming from a small rural school to this institution was a miracle.

Here I began to grow as a Christian. I joined a regular Bible study and obtained good Christian discipleship from the teachings in the school chapel as well. By God's grace I also had access to excellent sporting facilities. Swimming and hockey were my favorite sports and I also enjoyed camping. I learned first aid as well.

During the school holidays, which would normally be four-week breaks three times a year, I would go back home to our village, Ukia. I continued to be involved in teaching Sunday school, and I also became active in the local church's youth program. Our youth group was involved in evangelistic activities. We also organized youth rallies and invited guest speakers.

I clearly remember the joy of one such vacation. When I left school, I had a particular goal for my vacation: to be a blessing to my family. I was going to be a servant to them all. I would serve them as though I was directly serving God. And I did. I would be the first one to wake up and the last to go to bed. For the four weeks, I made an effort to keep the house as if Jesus would be coming by. Anything I did, I aimed at excellence. Every meal I made was done as if Jesus was our dinner guest. I also did laundry with extra care.

All of life is worship; the things we do or do not do are acts of worship. Indeed our choices reference who we worship.

This vacation was a life-changing experience for me. I confirmed what someone has said: all of life is worship to God. The things we do or do not do are acts of worship. Indeed our choices reference who we worship. Investing time in a service that glorifies God gives us great fulfillment in life. I went back to school a fulfilled girl and ready to do it again the following vacation.

Then God spoke to me one time about the things I chatted about, the idle talk with friends that was not exactly godly. It was not seasoned with salt as God expects of us. It was replete with lies and exaggeration to spice up the conversation. I felt that some of the stories I told would make Jesus move away because they did not reflect the fruit of the Spirit. Determined to change, I committed myself to be a silent observer and use that time thinking about how I should improve my speech. And so I became a listener to my friends, and through them learned much about what had been coming out of my mouth. For about a month I spoke very little, asking God to purify my speech.

I look back on those high school years as the time when God began to manifest His call on my life. He had a firm grip on me, causing me to consciously choose to follow Him. At the same time, He was equipping me because He had set me aside for His purpose. He knew what He was doing all along. It was all about preparing me for the purpose He wanted to accomplish through me.

For I know the plans I have for you declares the Lord, plans to prosper you and not to harm you, plans to give you hope and a future.   —*Jeremiah 29:11*

Chapter 3

Nailed to a Call

On completing high school and making a covenant with God to serve Him, I started a new chapter in my life. I stayed with my big sister Ruth in the city of Nairobi. I wanted to work, and I had a specific employment field in mind. I wanted to work in a bank.

I made applications and as I waited for the responses, I decided to go off for a one-week Christian youth camp organized by Word of Life. At that camp, I committed myself to start memorizing Scripture, a practice I have enjoyed and benefited from to this day.

While at the Word of Life camp, I met Victor, who became a special friend. He had lost his sight at a young age and had grown up blind. Victor was a good Christian, a very hard working undergraduate student and was in his first year, studying to be a lawyer.

I was attracted to him. He was good in music and played the guitar. He was also fun to be with and told stories all the time. I could not understand why God had allowed this impairment in his life.

Talking to Victor over tea break, I shared with him that I was hoping to join the same university he was in to pursue medicine. Then I made a commitment to him. "Once I get to college, I will be one of your reading helpers." He quickly told me he was appreciative of my desire to help, but that medical school kept people so busy, I would not be able to do that. I, however, meant what I said and prayed that God would allow me to do it some day.

After camp, I went back to my sister's house in the city. I was surprised that I still had not received any job invitation. This was not coming as quickly and as easily as I had anticipated. So I got in touch with some brokers, mainly relatives or their friends, who were well connected to hasten the process. Day after day, I got promises and new contacts. After eight weeks of this frustrating process, gastritis set in. This, together with the effect of my father's death, began to make me depressed. I needed a father figure to lean on in my life.

I decided to give up my job search and go back to our rural home. My plan was to serve in the church and at home until God opened a door for me to get a job. This decision gave me enormous peace. I wished I had done that earlier. Why did I not ask God in the first place what He wanted me to do rather than leaning on my own understanding, I wondered. Unfortunately, this is a mistake I have repeated so often in my life.

Why did I not ask God in the first place what He wanted me to do?

In the village I soon began to feel lonely and really missed my dad. I chose to spend a lot of time in prayer and soon began to relate to God in a very close way, as my Father. And He was a Father. I had no one to compete with for His attention. I would talk to Him about everything and listen to His guidance, which I so much needed. I would go for long walks and invite Him to come along with me. I would speak to Him as if He was human, walking by my side.

A seasonal river passes through in a valley close to our home. I would walk there and sit by the flowing water, praying and listening to God. He and I became great friends. I was so glad I had failed to get the job at the bank and was even happier being away from the hassle of city life. Little did I know God wanted me to go back home for that season so that He and I could get to another level of friendship. And all this was setting the stage for greater things to come later.

A few weeks after I returned home, I learned that the neighboring girls' boarding high school needed a Biology and Chemistry teacher. It was a ten minute walk from home. After consultation with my heavenly Father, I quickly took up this assignment. During the week, I would work as a teacher. Most evenings would be spent with the school girls in discipleship discussions and other extra curricular activities.

I started a guide/rangers club, which became such fun. We would travel to the hills with the girls, for weekend camp and learned life skills for self-development. I became the Christian Union patron and we would have lively praise and prayer times with the girls, as well as outreach activities.

One particular girl became a close friend. Her first and middle names were similar to mine. She was also a wonderful Christian with a pleasant character. I enjoyed our times of sharing and our friendship lasts to this day.

Being in the rural setting was a great time to learn to share, especially to meet the needs of the poor. I gave financially and materially to the old and needy. I would receive my salary and begin to pray that God would bring people in need to me. I experienced the joy of giving. I had no bank account, and I neither saved nor invested. I just gave.

I taught in that school for about one and a half years. College entry was delayed because of the political situation in the country and so all I had to do was wait. I did not know what I would take in college, although medicine was my first choice.

During that waiting period, I met a handsome young man, David, who had been a favorite student of my father. When he joined high school, my father had helped pay his school fees. He had gone on to develop a career in electrical engineering. Based on his good reputation, especially with my family, we began to date.

Soon afterwards, the situation in the country became favorable and the university was re-opened. I was admitted to the medical school, something I knew God was using to prepare me for the ministry.

Once I joined the university, the first person I looked for was Victor, my blind law student friend. I let him know I was ready to read for him. Two evenings every week were spent reading for him, and this went on until he graduated from the School of Law three years later. That was a wonderful time of ministry and I felt very privileged to share the sight God had blessed me with to help one who could not see.

During one of the college breaks in the first year of medical school, I traveled back home to rest and take time to pray. The pressure of medical school had interfered with my fellowship with God. Little did I know God was setting things up to speak to me yet again.

First, I was off for a week-long youth camp which turned into a refreshing time in the Spirit. At the end of the week, a teaching on baptism was given. I clearly understood that I needed to go through baptism by immersion. Thus, I sought to be baptized a second time as my initial baptism had been by sprinkling.

This did not bring much joy to my family, especially to my mother. She had recommitted her life to Christ after the death of my Father and was active in our local church. My aunt, who had been my godmother, was also not pleased. I respected and greatly admired my aunt, so this affected me too. For two days, I felt depressed. I prayed and cried to God to help me.

Then He spoke to me and told me that I was to "die" to my preferences, my tastes, my will, — "die" to the world and what it values. I was to die to the opinions of my family and only seek to work for His approval. So I went ahead with the baptism to fulfill all righteousness through a public declaration of my faith.

> *Do your best to present yourself to God as one approved, a workman who does not need to be ashamed, and who correctly handles the word of truth.*
>
> — *2 Tim. 2:15*

Reflecting later, I felt that this decision was a test from God. What followed soon after revealed my whole life's purpose.

At that time, the eastern part of the country where my home is located had been hit by a severe drought. Rain had failed for two consecutive seasons and people were in need of food.

Since I was on break, I would stay home when my younger sisters went to school and my mother attended her shop, a business she was running to generate income for the family. I would enjoy long quiet times, receiving spiritual nourishment.

One morning, about a month after my baptism, I had an unexpected guest, an old woman from the neighborhood. Her husband had been an alcoholic and had recently died. I was busy cleaning a portion of the backyard when I looked up, and there she was standing a few yards from me. I had not heard her coming, and our dog had not even barked at her.

As is the custom in my home area, she greeted me and I responded. I waited to hear her reason for coming to our house and she was quick to state it. She was sick and wanted some food. Her legs were swollen and peeling. Her face was also showing signs of puffiness. She walked with the help of a walking stick.

An overwhelming feeling gripped my heart. I still feel it to this day every time I see the sick and hungry. It must be a manifestation of compassion. I wanted to hug her. I wanted to take her in my arms and serve her. A very strong desire to care for her ran all through me. Tears filled my eyes and words failed me. I sensed a strange tightness in my throat that did not allow me to speak. I must have stared at her for an uncomfortable length of time as she went on to explain how she lived alone with no one to help. Then she asked if I could give her leftovers from breakfast.

In response, I invited her inside the house and warmed some food for her. I placed it before her and asked if we could pray together before eating. She was surprised that I would ask this because her family was not Christian; but she complied, perhaps in appreciation of the food before us. I prayed briefly and then gave her the opportunity to eat. Within no time, she had cleared what was on the plate.

Even after she left, a deep emotion remained in my heart. I could not do anything productive that day. I kept wondering what she could have done, had she not found me home. My heart was touched by the thought of people who suffer and die alone. I suddenly realized that the things that God has provided for us, and we tend to take for granted, are extraordinary and beyond reach for many people. I did not sleep very well that night.

The next day I was home alone again, and at about the same time, I heard the dog barking. I knew we had a visitor, and my immediate thought was that the same woman had come again. But I was wrong. On coming out of the house, I came face to face with a middle aged man who stood in front of our house, smiling. I knew him, and had seen him often in the market. He was deaf and dumb. I signaled to him to find out what he wanted. He asked for something to drink, and also for money. He showed his empty shopping bag and bare pockets and signaled he wanted something to buy food.

To my great amazement, the same overwhelming feeling came back to me afresh. I gave him something to drink and filled his bag with corn, potatoes and fruit. He was very thankful and expressed his gratefulness with all sorts of gestures. Then he left.

On the third day, at about the same time, a young boy came to our home. He had lost his mind. He had been going to school but had dropped out due to a psychiatric problem. I didn't actually hear him come; I suddenly noticed a figure silhouetted against the window, only to look up and see him peeping into the room.

I went out to talk to him. He was sober and responded to my greeting and questions like where he had been and how his family was. He told me he would like to go back to school but needed help. On further probing, he still remained silent and unfriendly. I asked him if he wanted to be well and on hearing that, he screamed and ran away. I later met him by the road with a friend of mine who is now a Bishop. We laid hands on him, cast the demon out and he became normal again and went back to school.

I knew that God was speaking to me through these experiences. I began to pray and it became clear that God was calling me to help the needy. God began to reveal the ministry He had for me.

My prayer in response to this November 1984 experience was simple: "God, give me a soft heart for men and women in need. Give me compassion that will prompt me to action, a love to love unto death as you did. Give me a heart that burns to evangelize, but before you send me, fill me completely with Your Spirit."

I reminded God of the covenant I had made with Him three years before. He had now called me to a multi-faceted ministry: To feed the hungry, to treat the sick and to set free the spiritually bound. While I didn't have the right word for it then, I now understand it to be wholistic evangelism. I committed myself to that call and to fulfilling it by His grace. Again, I asked God to cause me to fulfill it.

Now I realized that my purpose in medical school was to be equipped in order to use my medical degree as a tool for His glory. The location was soon revealed. That same year, the media carried pictures of children dying of hunger in the neighboring country of Ethiopia. The thought of such kind of suffering brought back the same feeling I had felt when I met the three guests whom God had used to speak to me about the ministry He was giving me. With this, I knew that God was asking me to go meet the needs of those suffering in Ethiopia.

And so, I decided to go to medical school to be equipped and then proceed to Ethiopia to serve as a medical missionary. Convicted, I returned after the six-week vacation to medical school to continue with my first year program.

Chapter 4

God's Interventions

In the years immediately after independence, rural Kenya where I grew up was replete with cultural practices that were unchristian. Witchcraft, for instance was common practice. Witches were known to give unsuspecting children food items to cause them harm.

With this awareness, and as a caring parent, one of the things my father insisted on when we were growing up was that we should never eat food given to us outside the home. This was often repeated to us — we were not allowed to visit just anyone. We were to stay home when not in school or church, eat at home, and be content. Permission had to be sought to attend functions, and instructions were always given about precautions to take when we got out there.

Obeying the instruction never to eat food away from home saved my brother and me on one occasion. We were looking after our cows when a neighbor stopped by and said she had something special to give us to eat. She handed us freshly baked *chapati* (Indian Naan like bread). It smelled delicious and was very timely now that it was about eleven o'clock in the morning. She ordered me to give half of it to my brother who was looking up with expectation. I followed her instructions and handed my younger brother his piece but also nudged and winked at him not to start eating before further instructions.

Once our "generous" neighbor had left, I took the chapati from my brother and explained why we could not eat it. He started crying for it, demanding I allow him to eat. But with a firm no, I tossed both pieces into the bush. Immediately, our dog went after the bread and gulped it. That made my little brother even angrier and he cried all the way home.

By the time we got to the house, which was only a short walk away, our dog was vomiting seriously and soon fell down frothing at the mouth. It remained unconscious for most of that day, although eventually it recovered. Our lives were spared but we were greatly scared. Dad used the incident to re-emphasize his counsel about the need to be cautious. Indeed my respect for his counsel went a notch higher.

Another intervention came when I was in first year of medical school. I had been dating David for about a year, having developed a relationship with him when I did a teaching job. He was not a practicing Christian although he occasionally joined me for Sunday worship services. He did not raise any objection to my convictions, and he did not object when I spent weekends on trips to high schools for rallies and ministry.

The first realization that this relationship was affecting my relationship with God came when I went with two other college mates to minister in a high school Sunday program. I was to share briefly after the message to challenge the students to respond and develop a personal relationship with God.

When I stood to share, I was gripped with shame and fear. I had no courage to urge or encourage. I noticed the dress I was wearing was shaking and I was inconsistent in my talk. I hurried to finish what I was saying and sat down, knowing very well that the boldness for the gospel had been overtaken by compromise. The Holy Spirit's power had faded.

When I returned to college, I found David waiting for me, and to my surprise, I realized I had no courage to push him out of my life. I even began to see him more often, further cutting off time I would have otherwise spend in ministry outreach.

David was an exceptionally good person. He treated me with respect. He honored my relationship with God and made sure he did not do anything that would be considered sin in my presence. So, I did not have any reason to stop seeing him! I was so infatuated by this relationship that I allowed him to give me all sorts of gifts. Before I knew it, I had accepted a ring from him. I felt powerless and trapped and I did not have time in between to think.

When he proposed to me, I did not have the courage to say no and so we prepared to have an official engagement. This meant a trip to my rural home in Ukia where his relatives would meet mine, share a meal, exchange gifts and agree to a relationship between the two families, based on our relationship. Thereafter we could proceed with wedding plans within six to twelve months.

In between all this, I would sense the gentle Holy Spirit letting me know I was making a big mistake, but I would quickly present my case, stating what a wonderful man David was and how he would become a Christian in no time. Finally the week we were to travel home for the official engagement arrived. I was both fearful and excited, all the time avoiding praying about this because I knew God might stop me.

David was out of town for work that week but he was to return the day before our trip. He had promised to come pick me up so we could go shopping before the trip home and I waited as agreed. When he failed to come, I thought he might have been delayed, so I decided we would skip the shopping arrangement. I went on to get packed in order to be ready to leave when he came.

Hours later, I was still in my college boarding room. I missed dinner as I waited and wondered. By that time, I calculated that people were already expecting us to be about to arrive at my home, which was about a two hours drive.

A knock on the door quickly had me respond to one of my college mates. She informed me that two people wanted to see me in the lobby of the university residence hall. I went down to meet them and they had a message from David. He had been involved in a road traffic accident that morning and had been brought to a city hospital by helicopter. He was going to be operated on that night and was requesting if I could visit him the next day.

That Friday night was one of the longest and most confused nights I had ever had. I was up early to go to the hospital. I saw him in hospital the next day, Saturday, the day we were supposed to be officially engaged. He was in pain and pinned to a hospital bed with a traction to his hip. He had a compound fracture to his femur along with other soft tissue injuries. He was to be in the hospital, in that position, for at least a month!

With David chained to a hospital bed, God began to talk to me. He now had my attention. I had ignored Him and taken a way I should never have taken. He began to woo me back to His way. I woke up to the remembrance of God's mission in my life and the covenant I had made with Him as I graduated from high school. I remembered my call to wholistic ministry. I refocused on the reason I was in the medical school. It was a painful "trip" back.

God's love for us is deep and He is faithful to His covenant. His ways are always best.

I needed to talk to a mature Christian, and God led me to a brother whose name was also David. I shared all I had been through and asked him to pray with me. It ended up being an entire night of prayer. As I repented and called on God to heal me, I was spirit-filled, spoke in a foreign tongue like the day of Pentecost, and my joy of salvation was restored.

How I had missed that fellowship with God! It felt so sweet to rest in Him again, forgiven and deeply loved. I had been tempted, and the call of God would have been sacrificed, had He not reached down to rescue me. He was faithful to the covenant we had made and exploited the permission I had given Him to cause me to remain on course.

My only regret was that David had been hurt in the course of it. And God was to quickly tell me why. By the time David was out of hospital, I had been restored spiritually. I had the courage to break the relationship. I had the strength to explain I was on a different path, headed in direction that was different from his. Had I been the one in hospital, receiving David's care and support, disengagement would never have been possible. Painful as it was for him, and for me, I was able to stop our dating, remaining as friends and seeing each other occasionally during family functions.

I also learned firsthand that I serve a jealous God before whom we cannot afford to have other gods. God's people cannot afford to worship an idol. God does not take it kindly when we have an idol in the form of anything to bow to or to worship. He said it to Moses and had him write it in the law He gave to the Children of Israel:

> *"... for I the LORD your God, am a jealous God..."*
> — *Exodus 5: 9(b)*

I am ever so thankful that God intervened at the right time, having patiently waited for me to turn back to Him. His love is deep. He took me in, healed my wounds, revived my soul and sent me onward in the mission journey through medical school.

Chapter 5

Equipping

From the middle of my first year in medical school, I knew God had me in the university to be equipped for ministry. That did not mean I was to stay idle. I was reading for my blind friend twice a week, but I desired to help other people in disadvantaged situations, too.

God does not call us to all people but He does place specific ones along our paths for relationship and ministry.

I became friends with a disabled girl with whom I spent time in fellowship. We would walk to and from the Christian Union meetings. I also attempted, but failed-to befriend my roommate who was also disabled. That bothered me, and many times I would pray that we would be friends but it never happened.

This made me realize that God does not call us to all people. He places some people along our paths for relationship and He is the one who opens their hearts to accept us. Some we desire to reach with love but they do not open their hearts or even welcome God's love through us, so they reject us. It pained me to be rejected, but I learned to accept it.

I have revealed you to those whom you gave me out of the world. They were yours; you gave them to me and they have obeyed your word. — *John 17:6*

The Christmas carol service that first year in college was memorable. I was asked to participate by doing a reading. Interestingly, I was asked to read Isaiah 61. Reading out of this passage to the Christian population in the university made me feel God's confirmation of what He had called me for. That was victory for me as I sensed the power of the Word. The first verse of that passage especially spoke to me.

The Spirit of the Lord is upon me, because He has anointed me to preach the good news to the poor. He has sent me to bind up the broken hearted, to proclaim freedom for the captives and release from darkness for the prisoners.

— *Isaiah 61:1*

Soon after this service, a family friend who was studying architecture at the university visited, wanting to talk to me. I harkened to his request, sensing he had something important to tell me. To have the opportunity to talk, we went out on a coffee date. He was straight in his talk. He was not a Christian and without mincing any words, he went ahead to let me know that being a Christian should not be viewed as everything. According to him, I still had a life to live and I needed to have fun. He advised me to use my time wisely, studying and having good times of relaxation. To him, good times were anything but helping people like my blind friend, going to high schools for missions during the weekends or studying the Bible. He went into great pains to try and convince me that I was wasting what would have been otherwise very exciting times.

I listened. He talked.He expressed concern, reasoning that he talked to me as a big brother would talk to his little sister. For some reason, I became emotional and cried. I don't remember why but he dried my tears with his shirtsleeve, consoled me and took me back to the residence halls, convinced he had helped me. To him, he was expressing a very sincere concern.

Much later after college, I ran into this friend at a family function.

He has become a very successful professional in our country and financially well off. We had another coffee date about ten years after the first one. He wanted to know what I was doing in Ethiopia. Was I working for UNICEF, or was it the UNFPA? He was shocked and deeply affected to know I was serving as a missionary among the poor. It was his time to cry as he felt "guilty" that he had not helped me and he felt he had failed to rescue me from a path that was leading to failure and he now felt guilty about how I had turned out. That is when I realized that the worldly definition of success is totally different from success in the eyes of God. The Bible states this very plainly: Godly things are foolishness to ungodly people and they cannot understand them.

The man without the spirit does not accept the things that come from the Spirit of God, for they are foolishness to Him, and He cannot understand them because they are spiritually discerned.
— *1Corinthians 2: 14*

I was blessed with unique opportunities to help others in college. One of these was a classmate. Because he was supporting his brothers and sisters in school, he could not use his student allowance money to buy good clothing and shoes. Having been poor and lacking many things when I was growing up, I could understand his need and was compelled to help. One time after our allowance was released, I went off to a shoe shop and bought him a pair of shoes. I left them in his room with a note that they were from a loving friend. He suspected it was me, and he wore them that same night to the library where we often met for group discussions. It was such a joy for me to see him feel good about that.

My blind friend Victor was often the recipient of my good deeds. I especially remember finding him one evening taking a nap as he waited for our reading time. He had a much worn out bedcover and the next day found me shopping for a warm woollen bedspread. I loved giving and counted it as a privilege to have an opportunity to do it.

As I envisioned the time when I would be in Ethiopia involved in working with the poor, the theme of my prayer changed, focusing on that country. One day, a friend of mine told me she knew of an Ethiopian lady named Hirut, who lived in Kenya. I became even more interested when I learned that she was a fifth year medical student in the same medical school I was in. I planned to meet her and we got together.

~~~

The world applauds people for what they have, are, or do, but our true home is in heaven and our values should be based on that culture. Make kingdom work a priority.

~~~

No sooner had I finished sharing my dream with her than I began regretting why I had done it. "Ethiopia is no place to dream of going, especially for a Kenyan," Hirut told me emphatically. "You people in Kenya are used to peace and are also familiar with prosperity, things foreign in Ethiopia," that she added.

In a nutshell, what Hirut said completely discouraged me. She did, however, invite me to come to her room the next Sunday evening for a 'taste' of Ethiopia. She set before me traditional food direct from her parents back home. That is how I ate *Injera* (fermented pancake-like bread) with a spicy chicken sauce for the very first time, served in her college room.

Six years later, I met Hirut in America. She had married and was practicing medicine. Meanwhile, I was raising support to go to Ethiopia with my family. It was a wonderful reunion. This time around she was an encouragement. Ethiopia was experiencing peace, regimes had changed and persecution of Christians had stopped. Hirut has become a prayer partner for our work and a great encourager.

My greatest spiritual achievement in my years of clinical training was having a prayer partner. I was attracted to Tabitha early in high school, but we never really got to talk much as she was quiet and reserved. She would often be alone and missed many meals, which cut her off from social engagements. I later learned she was committed to intercession, leading a life characterized by prayer and fasting.

In medical school, Tabitha was pursuing pharmacy. I learned of her prayer ministry through a friend and sought to partner with her. We began to meet twice a week in her room where we would pray for an hour or so. This became more frequent and we began to have days of fasting together. Through her I learned about the ministry of intercession.

For two complete years before she graduated from medical school, I had the wonderful privilege of being discipled in prayer by this woman of God. Then she disappeared from my life and I missed her a great deal. After raising my support to go to Ethiopia, I spent two weeks in Kenya. During that time, I tried to look for her but surprisingly, God did not bring us together again. It wasn't until recently, twenty years after those college sessions, that we met again. The deep walk she has with the Lord is due to her consistent prayer life. You can't help but notice the power of God in her.

Thankfully, God provided other prayer partners when Tabitha and I were apart. As soon as I arrived in the mission field, I met another "Tabitha." Her name was different but Yenenesh's style of prayer, her interest in me, and commitment to prayer were the same as I had seen in Tabitha. She became my "Tabitha" away from home; and to this day, we still meet and pray several times a week, either on phone, email or in person. We also fast together often. She is now not only a partner in prayer but also a partner in ministry.

Another dear prayer partner has been Emily, based in Nairobi, Kenya. Like Yenenesh, she and I have become connected deeply for several years now in the matters of prayer and following after Christ.

Prayer meetings have always held a special place in my life. One night during my fourth year in medical school, my younger sister Rose and I went off to an overnight church prayer meeting. I had joined a new church, the Nairobi Pentecostal Church and was beginning to enjoy it alot, even though I did not know many people there.

The prayer meeting had two sessions. The first one ran up to midnight and the second one started after a thirty-minute coffee break and went on till morning. During that coffee break, a friend of mine introduced me to Festus who was working for an airline as an accountant. We talked briefly and soon went in for the second session. At dawn, just as we left, I met Festus again and briefly visited with him before breaking off for the day.

The next Sunday after church, he came over to greet me and soon we became close friends. Two of his friends were already good friends of mine and so we quickly formed a team, developed a relationship and soon started dating.

At the end of the year, I started getting ready to leave the city for a medical elective term. This was to last three months and I chose to do it in a very remote area of northern Kenya, in a small missionary clinic among the Turkana people.

There were two reasons why I chose this location. One was to get away from Festus and have time to seek God to know if He was in this. I was determined not to make a serious mistake again. Secondly, I wanted to experience medical missions to have a taste of what the future had in store.

Seintje, a Dutch missionary nurse, was my hostess and we immediately became friends. She was single and had served in this remote area for about five years. Her relationship with God was deep and her ministry was closely linked to the church. She served a very needy community and she became a wonderful example for me.

Earlier in the year, before I took this elective, God had spoken to me very clearly. I was studying in my room and I felt prompted to walk to the window and look out. When I did, I saw a small aircraft taking off from an airport that was located on the same side of town as our medical school. It flew towards where I was and then turned north. The Spirit of God impressed upon me there and then the fact that I was going to be traveling around the world, and that I was going to start flying out that year!

When I first met Festus and found out that he worked for an airline, I thought perhaps there was a connection with what God had said, but that wasn't the means God was going to use to get me in the air. The elective term to the Turkana people became the connection. I flew there on a small police aircraft, taking off from the same airport and heading north. I seem to have been on the move since that moment, with flights beyond what I can keep count, to parts of the world I never imagined. God does have a sense of humor! I call the unforgettable moment when He speaks altar-building occasions.

Before I left for Turkana, Festus asked me to take time to seek God about His purpose for our friendship. This confirmed what was on my mind. He wanted us to discuss this when I got back. So, this was a second reason to seek God, I made it clear to him that I would pray.

I sought God. I wanted a sign from Him. One evening I walked to a hilltop in that semi-arid desert region to pray, just as the sun was setting. The Turkana landscape is beautiful with sandy brown fields and small rocky hills. It is sparsely populated and I enjoyed prayer walks and moments of meditation alone. On this particular evening, I felt very close to God and I wanted Him to speak to me.

He did and He gave me a sign to look for. If Festus would agree to come to this location and walk up that mountain with me, then he would also walk down the aisle with me. That would be the sign. I took this further: if Festus would come to Turkana with me, he would also walk the ministry road with me. Feeling I had found my answer, I descended from the hill to the house that had become my home.

Seintje and I shared devotions and singing together in the evenings. She taught me an old Christian hymn that still moves me to tears every time I sing it.

1. From heav'n You came, helpless Babe,
   Enter'd our world, Your glory veiled;
   Not to be served, but to serve,
   And give Your life that we might live.

   This is our God, the Servant King,
   He calls us now to follow Him;
   To bring our lives as a daily offering
   of worship to the Servant King

2. There in the garden of tears,
   My heavy load He chose to bear;
   His heart with sorrow was torn,
   "Yet not My will, but Yours," He said.

3. Come, see His hands and His feet,
   The scars that speak of sacrifice;
   Hands that flung stars into space,
   to cruel nails surrendered.

4. So let us learn how to serve,
   And in our lives enthrone Him;
   Each other's needs to prefer,
   For it is Christ we're serving.

   By Graham Kendrick ©1983 Kingsway's Thank you Music.

I spent three months in Turkana for the medical elective term. Those were three beautiful months of ministry, worship and growth. By the time I was ready to leave, Seintje had become such a dear friend, we were almost family. Using a simple sewing machine and working late at night she made me two beautiful dresses, giving these to me as a gift when we parted. She then drove me back to medical school, a two-day journey, and even visited my mother's house in the countryside, and stayed overnight. Bringing those whom I consider dear friends to the place I grew up is always very special for me.

A few months after I had returned to college, Festus proposed to me on a coffee date. By then, although I was convinced I would marry him, I did, however, have reservations. Would he come with me to the mission field? Would we walk up the hill in Turkana, symbolizing our joint commitment to the mission field?

In response to his request for my hand in marriage, I let him know I had made a covenant with God. I had said yes to a call for ministry to Ethiopia, and that is where I was headed sooner or later. If this was not something he could accept and be willing to be a part of, then marriage would not work for us. If he were to marry me he would have to be willing to 'marry' the call in me as well.

After a few days, he was convinced he wanted to serve God with me, wherever and whenever that would be. I then agreed to marry him once I was through with medical school. I still had a year of school, followed by an even more intense one year medical internship. But I was also watching. Would I see the sign?

The following month turned out to be very involving emotionally. I was to travel to Turkana to visit my friend Seintje. Festus wanted to come, and I thought this could be the time to see God confirm him as my future partner. We traveled by road on a public bus and the trip was very exhausting. By the time we arrived on the evening of the next day, Festus was down with a flu.

For most of our week-long stay in Turkana, he was miserable and hardly related with my friend. In fact she was convinced he was not the right person to marry me. On the final day, I mentioned I was going for a walk up the hill. To my surprise, Festus, who had been sickly, not eating and weak, decided to come with me. We walked up the small hill and back. God had confirmed He was for our marriage and thus nullified every other counsel.

Festus and I left the next day for the two-day trip back to Nairobi.

Half-way back, we had a stopover to change buses. During that break, Festus let me know he had decided to call off our relationship. It was over between us. I was numb.

This took me back to the advice my friend Seintje had given. She had clearly said she did not believe God had called us to marriage. Yet, the sign had been fulfilled and I had considered this as confirmation. Did I get it all wrong? Had I never learned God's voice? I thought I knew that voice and I thought I had clearly heard it! I read this part of His Word over and over again.

> *...His sheep follow Him because they know His voice. But they will never follow a stranger: in fact, they will run away from him because they do not recognize a stranger's voice.*
>
> *—John 10: 4-5*

I was distressed in the spirit. For several days, I could not eat or sleep well. I was crushed not so much because of the thought of the end of a relationship but the confusion as to what God was telling me. How do I follow the One who has called me if I cannot tell the difference between His voice and that of a stranger? And how was I then to go on? Had I been following a stranger all along?

A week later, on a Saturday, I took a day off and retreated to a lonely park. God and I talked and made a covenant once again. It was final; even if He was to slay me, I would follow Him no matter where or how.

When I got back to college that evening, a colleague, the one whom I had bought the pair of shoes brought me a note. It was from Festus. He had come to look for me but waited in vain. He wanted us to meet the next day after church and talk. He had realized he had made an irrational decision and wanted us to get back together again. After a while our relationship was healed and re-established.

Our time of courtship was not relaxed enough for romantic events as such. I was caught up in the busy schedules of medical school. On graduating as a general medical practitioner, I chose to do my internship in a town away from Festus' work. I did this in order to be able to concentrate and not feel guilty that I was not seeing him much. At the same time, we were busy with the wedding arrangements. Festus visited me often and God gave us quality times together.

The year went quickly. The wedding date was set and I was to relocate back to Nairobi so we could have our home there. So a week to our wedding day, I packed and set off for the city to begin a new life.

As I transported my belongings from my internship area to Nairobi on the eve of the wedding, we had a sad incident. We happened to stop the vehicle that carried my personal items — clothes, books and other household items — to go and eat, only to come back an hour later and discover that half of the things were gone. By God's intervention, however, the box that contained my wedding dress remained. Seintje had bought the wedding dress as a gift for my wedding in Holland. Most of my other clothes were gone.

What followed was a hectic time as we looked for a house and settled down in good time for the wedding. We got married in the same church where we had met and the hymn we chose for the great day told it all:

> Great is Thy faithfulness, O God my Father.
> There is no shadow of turning with Thee;
> Though changest not, Thy compassion, they fail not
> As Thou has been Thou forever will be.
>
> *Great is thy faithfulness! Great is thy faithfulness!*
> *Morning by morning new mercies I see;*
> *all I have needed thy hand hath provided;*
> *great is thy faithfulness, Lord, unto me!*
>
> Summer and winter and springtime and harvest,
> sun, moon and stars in their courses above
> join with all nature in manifold witness
> to thy great faithfulness, mercy and love.

Pardon for sin and a peace that endureth
thy own dear presence to cheer and to guide;
strength for today and bright hope for tomorrow,
blessings all mine, with ten thousand beside!

(Words: Thomas Chishulm, 1923)

For our honeymoon, we went to Mombasa by the Indian Ocean, after a night at a Christian guesthouse in the city of Nairobi. A new life had begun for both of us. Nine months later, our first son, Jay, was born.

Chapter 6

Beach Commissioning

Following our wedding, I reported back to work. The Ministry of Health transferred me to Nairobi where our new home was located. I became a medical officer in charge of health in a women's prison. This was such an eye opening experience!

I came to learn how women get involved in all sorts of crimes, for many reasons, including poverty, rejection, and unstable families. I met women who had killed, stolen, abused drugs or got involved in many other crimes. Women involved in prostitution were also locked up. I was able to connect and counsel with many of them. Several of these sought help because they had acquired HIV/AIDS.

What affected my feelings most were the children. Some babies had come with their mothers because they were breastfeeding, but some had been born in prison. I was often busy attending to the children when they fell sick. My heart had been touched by the condition of the children of Ethiopia before I went to medical school, and I was drawn to care about the well-being of these little ones as well. Consequently, I called for a meeting to drum up support for structural improvements that led to changes to the living conditions of children in that prison.

In addition, I began to think seriously about an idea that had begun to develop in my mind when I was in medical school – to pursue pediatrics and specialize in that area of medicine later at the postgraduate level. This was a natural fit for me and I felt that it would be just what I needed to do. Besides, specializing in the health of children, I felt, particularly now that I was six months pregnant, would help me in raising my children too. The maternal instinct in me contributed to convincing me that pediatrics is what God wanted for me. However, that would have to wait until our baby was born.

The gift of a child was simply overwhelming. As soon as I saw him, the agony of the prolonged labor was history. What a joy and fulfillment! Being a mother gave me a new sense of self worth and value. God affirms us in special ways that speak to us.

Our relationship with Jesus Christ should come first before other relationships or even a ministry.

I immediately realized, the challenge of my new status as a mother. I am convinced God used the responsibility of raising a precious child to train me for ministry. I learned it took courage to raise such a delicate, precious boy. It was also involving in that I had to get up at some odd hours when I would rather have slept. I also learned I could not ignore this boy for long; no matter how I tried, I was unable to. To some, I was termed over protective.

For instance, I remember the first time I left him home with a nanny to run an errand. I was so anxious to get home that I couldn't effectively attend to what I needed to do. As I left, I kept looking back to confirm that the house was not on fire. Later, I found that in the same way, ministry becomes precious to us. This also made me realize that Jesus should always be elevated above all these things, lest they become our idols. Our relationship with Christ should come first, before all other relationships even a ministry.

During Jay's first year, I took part-time work in private clinics and hospitals to supplement our income. Once when I was in one of those clinics, I learned that the provincial medical officer, who was my boss, was looking for me. As I called him from there, the secretary let me know how she had called every possible clinic in town looking for me.

I expected the worst. Was there an epidemic in the prison hospital, or was it a big emergency? Was the President coming to visit? The secretary had no idea why I was needed, and it took fifteen minutes before I could get connected to him. Meanwhile my stomach was in knots.

When he came on the line, however, he went straight to the point. He had been asked to propose a suitable candidate for a masters program in public health. There was a scholarship available from a development agency and the program was due to start in a week. He had proposed my name and I just had to take it. I was not allowed to object or give excuses. He was my boss, after all.

I was very surprised, more so because I kept hoping God would consider my desire to be a pediatrician. I did not want to waste time with a masters program that was not in line with His purpose for me. But, indeed, to my surprise, after talking to a few professionals, I realized this is exactly what I needed to be able to bring health care to communities. It was the perfect tool and God was handing it to me on a full scholarship. He always knows what we need even before we ask for it. The Word is true: He was in charge even when I thought otherwise. According to *Proverbs 21:2, the king's heart is in the hand of the LORD; he directs it like a watercourse wherever he pleases.* Simply put, God turns whatever authority is over us to be like water and makes it flow wherever he would.

My scholarship had many benefits attached to it. My research project was funded and so I was the first in my class to finalize the project. Also, since the donor had an interest in what I was research-ing, they funded a conference that brought together people to hear the presentation and discuss my findings. This led to changes in medical policy that benefited thousands of women in Kenya. Certain family planning services, for example, were to be provided by community health workers, making it possible for women to space their pregnan-cies without having to leave their villages to go for medical attention.

Wow! I had never planned for that, but God made it possible in such an awesome manner.

Following my graduation, I was offered a job by GTZ, the German development agency that had funded my scholarship. I gladly accepted, but God quickly "pushed" me out of there to pursue His plan through a job in an organization focused on providing services for the marginalized. When I started the two-year career with that organization, African Medical and Research Foundation (AMREF), I had no idea what God had in store for me.

Although I thought I was ready for the mission field, I came to learn that I needed to acquire certain skills and strategies that would prove useful later. AMREF reaches out to marginalized communities in several countries in Africa, and God made way for me to learn and develop skills under very special mentors. Within a short time, I had developed project management skills.

God also knew I would need to set up, train and equip teams at the community level and lead them. So He put me in a place to learn and implement several such projects, again working with people who had developed training strategies and teaching methodologies in this reputable organization. It was much more than I had anticipated.

Furthermore, I realized I needed training in disaster management as well as management of health emergencies affecting large populations. Before I even began to look for this kind of training, I was provided with scholarships to go to Switzerland, and then to Belgium, to learn. I was able to crown this education with a practical exposure to this kind of situation in Pakistan! What a favor from God!

During the "gold mine" time at AMREF, God again spoke. We were at a unique training conference in Mombasa, Kenya. Four community-based health care facilitators were training thirty participants. As one of the facilitators, I had a unique and profound experience right on the eve of this event. This was no ordinary group as the participants were church leaders drawn from the coast province of Kenya. They not only discussed health in its physical dimension but also talked of spiritual well-being. We shared in a wonderful participatory manner about what the Word of God commissioned them to do. My eyes were opened.

By the second day, I knew God was speaking to me. I took an afternoon to seek God in prayer and the reading of the Word. This took the evening and stretched into the night. Little did I realize that God been preparing me for a special experience the Sunday just before the conference. In the church service we sung a worship chorus:

We are standing on holy ground,
For I know that there are angels all around
Let us praise Jesus now,
We are standing in His presence, on holy ground.

> *(©1983 Meadow Green Music Co.)*

Tears began to flow down my face as I sensed the holy presence of God in a profound way. This set me up for the week.

That afternoon, evening and even during the night, as I spoke to God on the shores of the Indian Ocean, God reiterated the call to Ethiopia: *Establish a Christian health organization for My use, beginning in Ethiopia, to carry out a wholistic ministry like what was discussed this week in the conference! Your mission field will comprise the nations on the continent of Africa. Using the ministry, you will bring health to the poor through the local church. The organization will get its name from the theme of John 10:10, "...that they may have life and have it in abundance". Its purpose will be based on Psalm 96:3, "Declare the Glory of God among the nations, His marvelous deeds among all people".*

That was on April 18, 1993. On April 17, 2002, exactly nine years after God first spoke to me about this organization, Life In Abundance, (LIA) International, was legally incorporated as an organization in the US, having already existed as a ministry in Ethiopia for three years. God's timing is marvelous. To make this happen, however, God took me through experiences that I will share later.

I felt very comfortable working for AMREF and was learning a great deal and learning it fast. Doors of opportunity to learn kept opening and I knew it was a season of God's favor.

Earlier I had decided, and Festus had felt this as well, though reluctantly, that based on the life we expected to live in hardship areas, and much travel, raising one child was enough. God, however, let me know that He had a different plan!

I clearly remember the day. I was walking back to the office from lunch and it was like I was having an audible conversation with God. He told me I was being very selfish. I stopped right there by the road! Was what I had heard about the lunch? No! It was about Jay, our son. God told me that Jay was very lonely, yet I had selfishly been pursuing my self interest. Jay's loneliness would be even worse in remote areas so I had to have another child.

When things don't go as we expect, that doesn't necessarily mean that we haven't heard God's voice. We need to keep on in the task He has given us.

I guessed that my husband had been petitioning God about this. Whatever the case, I knew I could not disobey God!

I went ahead and conceived, but that pregnancy ended in a miscarriage eight weeks later, breaking my heart and throwing me into confusion over what God meant! I am yet to know why this happened because God's voice had been clear. Soon after, I conceived again and many blessings came about during that pregnancy.

Feeling all set now that the baby was growing well and nearing delivery, Festus and I began to feel strongly that the time had come to step out in ministry. God was set to intervene in a surprising way.

Chapter 7

Time to Go

God continued to stir us to move on. The equipping stage was over. We needed to step out of our comfort zone by faith and grab what God had prepared us for.

At about that time, the theme for the year in our home church, Nairobi Pentecostal Church, was, "There is hope for Africa." Pastor Dennis White, our Senior Pastor then, was urging the church to move beyond our borders. It couldn't have been more direct for us. Week after week, this was emphasized, making us more uncomfortable waiting.

We knew Ethiopia was our place of ministry. With this awareness, we began to search for connections in that country. It was then that I met a leading mission agency' development director on a flight. Jim was serving in Ethiopia at the time and, on hearing of our desire, updated me on the situation there.

Through my conversation with Jim who sat next to me on that domestic flight from Nairobi to Kisumu, I learned that rural Ethiopia was highly under-developed. It would therefore take a lot of will power to settle and minister there. I also learned of some local churches that I could work with. Armed with their addresses, I began to make inquiries through mail and even faxes, yet no response came back. After three months of actively searching for connections without success, Festus and I felt we might just need to leave for Ethiopia, search for jobs and begin ministering, somehow.

It was at the time when we were toying with this idea that I received a call at my work place through the switchboard. The caller, Greg, was an American, and he was serving as a missionary with Christian

Missionary Fellowship (CMF). He was working in Kenya and his organization needed assistance to set up a relief project to help the Maasai community with food. There had been a prolonged drought and many children were malnourished. Greg needed aid to carry out a nutrition survey.

Greg and I had a long discussion. He told me about his agency and I found out that they also worked in Ethiopia, which was what I most wanted to know. He also gave me the contact address for their Indianapolis office. I sent a letter to CMF the same day with a request to serve with their agency in Ethiopia.

A few weeks later, CMF responded. They needed Festus and I almost right away. First, they wanted us to fill in as short-term assistants in Kenya, working with the Maasai. A couple that had been serving there, who had similar resumes and experience as ours, was going on an extended furlough. Festus was to take charge of the administration while I was to provide oversight to five clinics. After this, we could then proceed to Ethiopia. What a perfect offer, or so it seemed.

Immediately after we got this information, I received yet another offer. I was invited by the UN to take up a position in Botswana, to to steer a national project in community based health care. The salary and the allowances were very attractive. They were very pushy. They kept calling and faxing every day to have my commitment. Meanwhile, every demand I made hoping to have a reason to say no was granted. This made me very confused. To make matters worse, when Festus told his bosses he was going to leave their organization, they offered him a promotion and increased his salary and benefits.

Everything seemed to be coming our way on a platter, and these opportunities looked very attractive. How could we say yes to CMF and no to these other offers? We began to think we could take these wonderful opportunities for a year or two and have the additional income be our start-up fund for missions. Logical thinking, isn't it?

At the same time, we got more information about the CMF package.

There was no salary attached to the job; rather, we were going to have to raise our own support. We would have to begin talking to friends and churches to have them commit to supporting us in missions. That sounded incredible. Most of the people we would be asking for support were serving in lower paying jobs than we were. Furthermore, it was not common among our people for successful career people to resign from their work and seek support to do ministry work. We had seen some people raising support, but most were evangelists, college students or non-graduates seeking to be in the ministry. The requirement for us to resign and start living on support to be in ministry sounded odd.

Undoubtedly the choices before us were really giving our human desires bargaining strength, making the option to continue with our jobs and go to Ethiopia later, more attractive. We could even go to Ethiopia using our own funds and one of us could continue working to supplement our financial resources in ministry there, we reasoned.

Working among the Maasai meant leaving our extended families and friends to go and live in a very remote environment. It also meant removing our first son from a good school and taking him where there would be no social amenities with home schooling as the only way to go (home schooling was and is not a recognized schooling option in our country's education system).

About that time, I delivered our second son. Since I had been traveling a lot during the pregnancy, we named him Kyalo, which in my Kamba laguage means a journey. Our first son had been named after Festus' father, Mwangangi which means one who moves from place to place.* At that time, we had no idea how prophetic these names would be for the lifestyle our children would immediately begin to live.

God was in business and He began to work on us. We continued to pray and wanted to hear a clear word from God to enable us to make our decision. Although the other jobs offered seemed the logical choice,

---

* Since it would have been disrespectful to publicly call out his grandfather's name we referred to him as Junior. The name was eventually shortened to Jay, his current middle name.

our hearts were not convinced to accept them. We felt the burden for the Maasai to be urgent and chose to go with CMF.

First, though, if we were going to be Christ's disciples, we needed to be able to count the cost.

> *If anyone comes after me and does not hate his father, mother, his wife and children, his brothers and sisters — yes, even his own life — he cannot be my disciple. And if anyone does not carry his cross and follow me, he cannot be my disciple.* — *Luke 14:26*

We were going to have to surrender our security. It was going to be God working through us, not us doing our own thing and periodically asking for His help. The self in us had to be crucified. We were to become like Christ, taking the path He took, letting go of every position and not grasping any for ourselves!

> *Your attitude should be the same as that of Christ Jesus. Who being in very nature God, did not consider equality with God something to be grasped, but made Himself nothing, taking the very nature of a servant, being made in human likeness. And being found in appearance as man, He humbled Himself and became obedient to death, even death on a cross.* — *Philippians 2:5-8*

The rest of the CMF affiliation process moved quickly. The last thing was an interview with their team leaders who were living in Kenya. We were invited for dinner after which an interview followed. It was wonderful as we sensed a confirmation in our hearts that we were embarking on what God wanted us to do.

As if to punish us for this feeling after making up our minds, Satan attacked that same night. We came home so full of joy and hope, convinced that God was leading us. Then our little one, who was now beginning to explore, tipped over a hot water kettle. Boiling water spilled on his hands and shoulder, causing large superficial burns. These are the most painful kind, although they heal faster with little scarring. He screamed all the way on the midnight ride to the hospital, where he was sedated for the night to facilitate treatment. What a contrast, from a decisive and joy-filled occasion at the start of the evening to a screaming arrival in a hospital casualty at midnight!

Delayed obedience is disobedience.

In spite of this setback, we quickly realized we had a clear choice to make. Delayed obedience was disobedience. It was either God's way or ours. We were either to hold onto these opportunities and lose, or we were to release them and gain. We chose to go. We submitted our resignation letters, burning the bridge of job security behind us.

We were able to raise some support in Kenya. Friends from the Christian Doctors' Fellowship helped. Our church also gave us support, though this was just a small percentage of the resources required for the work we were going to carry out.

To finalize the support raising process and the affiliation and commissioning for ministry, we were to travel to the United States, where CMF is headquartered. Once we were back from the US, we would move to Maasai land. We dismantled our household furniture, packed what could be stored and gave the rest away. We moved into a guesthouse briefly, then we left for the USA, knowing we would be coming back to Kenya, not to a home but to a mission field.

During the flight to the US, the reality of what we had done hit me. I suddenly realized that I did not have a home or a job to return to. My children did not have a home anymore or a kitchen to prepare their meals. I had an infant and here I was going to a culture that was foreign. I didn't even have an idea what would be available to feed him. My heart sank and I cried for a good part of that flight. The children were also air sick and the altitude changes hurt their ears, especially as we landed. By the time we arrived in the US, I was depressed.

But a pleasant surprise for us was to see that everything we needed was available in the US. The number of choices for one single product was overwhelming. Everything required a choice for brands or flavors!

We participated in a retreat aimed at giving missionary recruits an orientation to the new life style and its demands. In one of the sessions, we were directed to write all the things that mattered most to us in our former lives. We then shared in groups and prayed that we might release them. Then we did a literal release. Tying that list of the things we cherished on a helium balloon, we let it go. I watched my job and home rise into the air and fully surrendered myself to God. It was then that I "died" to the comforts that would hinder me. As Paul wrote:

> *But whatever was to my profit I now consider loss for the sake of Christ. What is more, I consider everything a loss compared to the surpassing greatness of knowing Christ Jesus my Lord for whose sake I have lost all things. I consider them rubbish that I may serve Christ.* — *Philippians 3: 7-8*

Support raising was successful. God brought a team to rally behind us to go to the Maasai. We were encouraged and after a three month stay in the US, we returned to Kenya and proceded to the Maasai land.

Chapter 8

Working among the Rural Poor

The Maasai are a well-known people of Kenya because of their out-standing culture which they have managed to maintain in the face of strong Western influence.

Their concentration is in two districts, Narok and Kajiado. CMF's ministries targeting the Maasai were based in the Narok district. In one particular location, CMF had established five clinics to address medical needs. Churches had also been planted in several areas of the region.

Our work there was to minister to the Maasai by caring for them medically through these clinics and also strengthening the church's role in reaching the community. All this we did from a remote location, about four hours drive from Nairobi, right inside the Maasai Mara national game reserve. We occupied a house that had previously been occupied by the missionary couple we were replacing.

We did not fully understand why we were doing this, or even how we could accomplish our task. Being a remote area, there were no schools, so I took on home schooling for our first born, then five years old, as well as caring for the smaller boy, then one.

There were no shops close by, so we traveled once a month to Nairobi to get our supplies. I sincerely hated these trips to town because they meant meeting former colleagues and having to answer questions that told us we were not understood and there was no good reason why we should be doing what we were doing. While we didn't doubt that we were in the place God wanted us to be, it was fruitless trying to justify our choices and new lifestyle to these people. Appearing in formal settings with the un trendy bush clothes made our friends wonder what had become of us.

Our two-bedroom house got its water from an open spring which flowed by gravity to a tank about two hundred feet from our house. We had a windmill that generated some electricity and we tapped this into a battery for use in lighting our house and a nearby clinic at night. We also had a socket in the kitchen from which we could run a TV and VCR. Part of the electric power was fed into a simple electric fence around our spring to keep animals off. Unfortunately this power source sometimes failed, and on several occasions elephants completely messed up the spring, making us go without water for days before it was fixed.

We cooked our meals on a gas cooker and had a kerosene-powered refrigerator which cooled food by a system that required a pilot light to be on all the time. When it went off after running out of kerosene, starting it again was a big hassle. Other times it would smoke and the fire alarm would wake us up in the middle of the night.

Living among the Maasai was interesting. They are a nomadic community and each home has a cowshed. The environment is therefore prone to flies. Moreover, they believe that to shew flies away is to shew away wealth. And so flies sit on children's eyes and mouths undisturbed. The Maasai share their water holes with their cows and their drinking water has a high concentration of animal urine, which they do not seem to mind.

Yet the Maasai are a very hospitable and friendly people. On many occasions, we were invited to their houses for dinner. Other times when we stopped by for a visit, we would be served tea and milk. The tea had the urine smell from the water. The milk usually would have a fly or two in it and, being served from smoked containers, it would also have charcoal particles. It was difficult to distinguish which were flies or charcoal.

A running stomach was the order of the day in our family. We also struggled with asthma which Kyalo developed as soon as we moved to the Maasai land. He would constantly get attacks, especially in the rainy season. This slowed his growth and affected his appetite; all he wanted was fruit juice. He also had an allergy to milk, making it even more difficult bringing him up in that area.

Festus served as the administrator for the clinics and was in charge of getting medical supplies from Nairobi. On several occasions, he helped transport patients to our referral hospital.

My role was to oversee the work in the clinics and consult with the nurses on any difficult cases. The main clinic was a three-minute walk from our house and I worked there daily. But at least once a week, I also drove across the park to visit the other clinics where I would see patients who needed a doctor. Usually these were the more serious cases the nurses could not manage.

Besides the clinics, I provided home schooling for Jay. This did not succeed because we lacked a good curriculum and guidance. There were also frequent emergency cases to attend to, which interrupted the study time.

I felt compelled to minister to the Maasai spiritually. I struggled with how I could bring together church ministry and the medical work to make it one ministry rather than a two-pronged ministry.

I began by holding heath education seminars for women desiring to teach them to value basic hygiene. I hoped to improve their personal hygiene, childcare and home care. I also taught them the importance of boiling milk before use to control brucellosis, which was one of the major illnesses among the Maasai.

Some of these seminars turned out to be hilarious. After the discussion on the importance of taking full body baths, one of the ladies, the Pastor's wife, committed herself to try it, although she had all sorts of reasons why bathing would be hazardous. She went home, warmed some water, put it into a basin and, going behind her house, took a full bath! She came about an hour late the next day for the seminar and disturbed the session! She could not wait to tell her story so I gave her the floor. Having taken a bath the previous night, she had slept so well that she actually believed she was in heaven. When she woke up in the morning, all she wanted to do was take another bath. So she made a thirty-minute round trip to get water, heated it and had a slow, enjoyable bath. Shiny and clean, she was now jumping up and down telling the story, confessing how young she felt! That started the bathing movement in the community.

Another moving story was from yet another woman. I was teaching about brucellosis and its relation to drinking unboiled milk, but no one in the audience would believe me! Suddenly, a woman stood up. She was furious that the other women were so hard to convince. This woman took the floor and challenged the women saying that she and her family always boiled milk and that for over two years since she started this practice, none of them had been down with the disease.

Slowly, we began to affect the health practices of the community. But our desire was to also see changed lives through the experience of salvation. We realized this needed to start within the workers themselves. Towards this goal, we initiated clinic staff retreats to build a spiritual accountability forum. A pastor from Nairobi visited during one of these retreats and taught on exemplary Christian living. Short devotions were held in the clinic before the start of each day's work.

A team came from a church in another part of the country and challenged the leaders towards worship, outreach and power evangelism. Some spiritual bondages and yokes were broken and we immediately began to experience a revival which spread to some of the other local churches we worked together with. I also began to hold Bible study in our house. Church leaders were challenged about personal commitment to Christ. We were very encouraged and witnessed commitment and growth in a new way.

Our ministry roles and experiences among the Maasai can be

summarized by this newsletter article we wrote in the middle of our stay there:

"To everything, there is time." For us, it has been a time of new beginnings and new insights and we feel the Lord training and teaching us. This makes us excited because we know the Lord has a task for which He is equipping us.

The most common question people ask is: "How do your different backgrounds merge to function in this medical and evangelistic ministry?"

When we took to medical missions, we also wondered how medical work was going to address evangelism and how our different backgrounds were going to apply on a day-to-day basis.

Festus' title in the ministry is administrator and he has a commerce and accounting background. Florence is the medical doctor in charge of the ministry, with a doctors' training and a specialty in public health. A recent happening here in the field demonstrated how this all works together.

We first met the Maitai family when they needed medical care for their one-week-old infant, Kipingot. Kipingot was seriously ill and when Florence saw him, he had a very high fever, was severely jaundiced and his whole body was swollen. He cried continuously, as if in pain. He struggled to breathe and refused to breastfeed. As it was already evening, we figured that a trip to our referral hospital two hours away wasn't the first choice, especially since we feared he would die on the way.

We gave him drugs to counter the overwhelming infection, and something for the pain and fever. We prayed with the Maitais and asked them to come the next day for more injections. When they left that evening with the baby still crying, we feared we would receive news of the child's death the next morning. That night we prayed for them. The continuous cry from Kipingot was so heart breaking and watching him struggle for breath made one wish they could breath for him.

The next morning, to our surprise and that of his parents, Kipingot was still alive! We noticed that his parents had shaved his head the previous night to prepare him for the funeral but because he was still crying continuously, they came.

His condition was not any better but we noted he was very dirty. Florence gave him a bath and put some of our son's clothes on him. He continued on the same medication for the rest of the day and by evening, he began breastfeeding.

The next morning, Kipingot had a shocking new development. His swelling had subsided, but he had developed painful abscesses all over his body and his clothes were soaked with pus. We couldn't believe this overnight development. He was, however, still feeding. So, puzzled as to what this could be, we continued treatment but tested the mother for HIV. She was negative, and we decided to refer the baby to hospital as soon as he was stable enough to make the trip.

The next morning threw us into even greater confusion. Kipingot's abscesses were worse. The skin around his shoulders and back had sloughed off, and he was discharging such foul smelling pus that everyone walked out of the clinic as soon as he was brought in! His shoulders and backbones were exposed and he had every reason to be a dead 10-day old boy, but there he was sucking on his mother's breast! We named him the "Miracle Baby".

Given his exposed bones, and the fact that our clinic was not equipped for in-patient care, we decided to risk the trip to our referral hospital, even though he was still not stable. Later that morning, Festus left for hospital with Kipingot's parents. Kipingot was padded with bandages all over his body, but still emitted a very foul smell.

The medical staff at the referral hospital found it very difficult to believe what Festus was telling them about Kipingot. They couldn't believe that he was only 10 days old, was coming from a village situation with rotting body tissues and exposed bones, and was still alive! They didn't even want to handle him much so they did their examination from the mother's lap. He was still alive though and could not be turned away, so he was admitted with his mother. Festus paid for his hospital care and left.

The hospital staff called us the next day over the radio saying the baby was worse, and the father should go as soon as possible so that he could come back home with the mother. They suspected he would die very soon. There didn't seem to be much hope and so Festus sent the father off to the hospital with some transport and pocket money.

Kipingot did not die then, so the father stayed for one week and then came home. After three months, Kipingot was discharged. He was not only spotlessly clean, but he was in perfect health, even tending towards overweight with full cheeks and a big smile on his face. It was a MIRACLE. When they came to our house on their way home, we saw why the Lord had placed us here with administrative and medical backgrounds. We prayed with them, thanked God together and sent them home with baby clothes.

Kipingot continued in good health, and started attending the well baby clinic for immunizations. His father sold a cow and promptly repaid all the financial expenses we had incurred. A friendship developed and every time the Maitais family came to the clinic, they would come to our house to visit and bring us some milk from their cows.

We wish we could just end this story here, but God had another development to it. About two months after Kipingot was discharged from the hospital, we traveled to Nairobi to replenish our household and medical supplies. When we arrived home we found that Kipingot had suffered overnight from diarrhea and vomiting, and had DIED! Our hearts were broken!

That same day we went to visit the Maitais to comfort and encourage them in the Lord and while there, we realized that the people in that village did not have a church. There were no practicing Christians there! We continued visiting and we were told that a church had been initiated in the past, but it had died.

With new vigor, that church has restarted! The Maitais have remained dear friends, and still visit us. We have also won other close friends from their village who are participating in the church.

Although Kipingot died at a time when we felt he had every reason to live, everything that took place brought glory to God!

All this made us grasp anew, that this work is the Lord's. He will use us to achieve His purposes in His way and time. Our job is to be available and obedient. What He chooses to combine in us and use will be for Him to decide. He is not limited to backgrounds and experiences. We serve a faithful God of new beginnings!

Our time among the Maasai was wonderful. It was a training ground for what we would experience in Ethiopia. One of the things we felt God wanted to show us was the fact that some of our fellow country men are highly disadvantaged, so that we do not look down on the Ethiopians when we got there. Our experience among the Maasai really humbled us.

Financial resources were a big challenge. Our ministry was not well supported. Everything we raised was spent on field expenses. For our supplies we begun to depend on our savings, which soon ran out. God, however, remained faithful and made sure we had enough to eat and had other necessities of life.

In the last quarter of our eighteen-month stay we wrote:

Looking back on our 15-month stay in Narok doing medical and evangelistic work among the Maasai, we can only thank God for the experience!

It has confirmed to us that we will be involved in ministry for the rest of our lives. Our job descriptions increased things we had not been trained for. We have been trained in many ways, and we have also grown in the faith.

God has been by our side and we have experienced His grace in times of trials. His guidance has been evident and we have had a fulfilling term.

Chapter 9

Ethiopia, Here We Come!

In the last month of our work among the Maasai, an offer was given to us. We could continue to serve in Kenya for another three-year term, this time in a central training center, where we would also begin some medical work. This was attractive to us in many ways. Festus would manage the center, and I would be able to learn a few more strategies before we proceeded on to Ethiopia. But what was God's will for us?

We took some time to pray about this option. I was more stressed than I initially thought. I so much wanted to hear God. Was it time to move on to Ethiopia or were we to wait a little longer?

On my third day of fasting, I still had not discerned God's will. I was in the room we used as Jay's classroom. It was mid-afternoon and Jay had taken a break. I looked out of the window, across the fields and up to the mountains. I then looked at the clouds just above the mountains and saw something incredible!

Right there in the clouds was a mountain! At first, I thought it was a reflection of the hills below, but on closer look, I realized it wasn't. Without even thinking, I took a pen and began to draw this image on the first page of my Bible which lay open on the "schoolroom" table. I did not draw just the outline but also added a few details. Before me I had a picture of the image I had seen. When I looked up again it was gone. It had vanished as quickly as it had appeared.

I was really amazed but excited. Actually I was beside myself with excitement. I took the Bible and ran off to Festus' office, which was on the east side of our compound. He could not understand a thing about what I was saying as I was so excited but couldn't find words to fully explain my experience and what it meant.

I wished I could restore the image I had seen for him to see. After some time, I composed myself and explained what had happened, yet I had no interpretation for it. What did it mean? I knew it was an answer to our prayers, but I had to trust God to explain it in His own way.

I sensed a profound, yet inexplicable peace, although I still did not know whether it was time to go to the long-awaited Ethiopia or not.

The team in Ethiopia had invited us to go and serve initially for a five-year term. We were to be involved in a ministry similar to the one we had served in among the Maasai. The medical and evangelistic ministry would be among the Gumuz people, an unevangelised tribe on the western side of the country. Festus was to do the administration work for the CMF office in Addis Ababa.

What stood in the way, however, was the fact that again we needed to raise the money for our projects. The first time we had gone to raise support had turned out to be very challenging and we were not eager to do it again. And now it would certainly be more difficult as it would mean being in the US for nine to twelve months.

To help us in making the decision, the team invited us to visit Ethiopia for three weeks. Leaving our boys with their grandparents in Kenya, we traveled to Ethiopia, now sixteen years after God had first spoken of a ministry to Ethiopia..

As we flew into Addis Ababa, I was on the lookout to see if the mountain I had seen was anywhere in sight in the country. But no, the landscape of the capital city had nothing even close to the image I had seen.

A few days later, after an orientation time in the capital, we took a small plane and flew to the community where we intended to do ministry. The area was very remote, only accessible by air. I wondered how the Mission Aviation Fellowship (MAF) pilot found his way over those mountains to his destination.

We landed on an unpaved airstrip, sending up a big cloud of dust. Once the dust had settled, we stepped out to be engulfed by 42 degrees C (nearly 108 degrees F) heat. We walked down the valley to the missionary house where an American couple in their late fifties were living. They had a clinic and a church, and had invited us to implement a community health program to reach the Gumuz people.

A tent was pitched for us where we would stay for five days. We went in to store our bags but came out almost immediately; the temperatures inside were unbearable.

As we sat down on a small wooden bench in the shade to rest, I looked up across the valley. I nearly fainted. Right there before us was a replica of the very image God had showed me earlier. I ran back into the tent and poured out the contents of my bag, looking for my Bible. When I saw it, I opened to the first page where I had drawn the image. Sitting there, we compared the details. It was indeed the exact reproduction of the image I had seen in the vision. Our God is amazing!

Now I knew! God had put up a clear road sign. The decision was made. He was simply saying, *this is the way*. This was an unmistakable sign that He was the one calling, and the good thing about this sign is that it would always be there as a reference, for times of doubt were to come later.

In working out His purpose in our lives, God is not in a hurry. We should not be discouraged if it takes many years to accomplish what He has laid on our hearts. Waiting time is not wasted time.

The rest of our stay was spent familiarizing ourselves with what was going to be Festus' responsibilities in administration, seeing the boys would be school, and interacting with our team mates. Before leaving, we had a team retreat at a lake near Addis Ababa.

Back in Kenya, we had a short family time visiting relatives, doing the handing over of our ministry among the Maasai, and saying our goodbyes. Our next destination was the CMF head office in the US to raise support in preparation for relocation to Ethiopia.

Just before we left for the US, I went looking for reference books that explained the link between community health and evangelism, in an effort to prepare a proposal for ministry among the Gumuz. I wanted a strategy that would address both physical and spiritual needs, making medical work an avenue for evangelism.

I had some know-how. AMREF had indeed been a gold mine of experience. I had taught trainers in community based development. The ministry of Jesus clearly communicated his way of ministering as he empowered his disciples to serve. But now was the time to structure a strategy. The pilot work among the Maasai had tested some of the initiatives I had in mind. I was now to write a curriculum that I could implement in Ethiopia.

God led me to the very book I needed, *Multiplying Light and Truth Through Community Health Evangelism,* by Stan Rowland. As I read it, all my remaining questions were answered and all my ideas were confirmed. The strategy I had in mind had actually been tested in the East African region. Using guidelines from this book, along with what I had learned from my public health training and practice, I put together a proposal for the Gumuz work and printed out the document to begin to solicit funds.

Our time in the US went well. We attended a very refreshing spiritual retreat for missionaries and God continued to give direction and insight. We traveled to different states but spent a significant amount of time in Kansas with what became our sending church, Cedar Ridge Christian Church. The church has remained very special to us to this day. I remember confessing before the elders in a very bold way that God was sending us on a big mission and they would be glad if they partnered with us. Well, after twelve years, that leadership came to see us in the field and certainly, God had actualized that confession. We built many other relationships with churches and families who remain dear to us.

In February 1998, God began to charge me to take full responsibility for the vision He had given me. He began to prepare a 'womb' in me of the birthing of this work. For my birthday, one of the Christian organizations I was working with gave me a cup with three inscriptions:

Leave the crowd
Look within
Let your dreams soar

This was a special inspiration and I began to revisit God's purpose in my life with added diligence. We received a prophecy that God would establish an organization for this ministry in the US. Four years later to the month, we had the joy of seeing this fulfilled.

Once a good percentage of our support was in, we left for Ethiopia arriving on August 10, 1998. A week later, we enrolled in language school to learn Amharic, the national language.

Our home was located on a missionary compound in Mekanisa, a poor area of Addis Ababa. Many Ethiopians who had been evacuated from Eritrea when the Ethiopia-Eritrea war broke out had been settled in this neighbourhood. The area was also next to the Alert Leprosy Hospital and many lepers and their families had settled nearby. Across the valley was the city dump and many people who lived off garbage also stayed here. Every day we drove through this community coming and going to language school.

Language study was a very humbling experience. It was a requirement of our mission agency to learn and use the language of the people we were called to. It was like learning to talk again! Although we were already fluent in three languages (English, Swahili, and Kamba), and had picked up Maasai as a fourth one, Amharic was in a class of its own.

As I struggled with the language, I could not help but imagine that I would be more useful practicing medicine and helping as I had come to do. I started by looking for a way to convince my missionary team to allow me to skip language learning. I thought of raising this as an agenda item in our first team meeting.

To my surprise, when we got the team meeting agenda, one of the items was the Muindis' language learning! I thought God had already heard my desire and acted. To my great surprise, however, when we came to that point, it was Festus alone who was allowed to cut short his language learning so that he could assume the field administrator's job. God has such a sense of humor! Festus was actually enjoying learning the language and yet he is the one who was excused. My attempts to be excused also were in vain. In fact, I was to be in language school for nine months since I would work directly with the community!

Surprisingly, the language learning time ended up being very useful to me. It helped me to slowly ease into the culture before jumping into activities. I am sure I was spared what would have been fatal mistakes in starting this ministry.

Satan began to attack. As we began to lay strategies for our ministry, I got an allergic reaction to something I could not identify. My face was swollen and blistered and it just kept getting worse. It lasted for weeks, making me very depressed because of my looks.

We also received discouraging news from home. My nephew had been severely burned and admitted in hospital. One of my brothers had been attacked by thugs and robbed at gunpoint.

But in spite of all these things, God continued to urge me on in the ministry. He revealed to me what was to be the initial logo of the ministry, talking of a time when we will take on a new logo. He also brought our way a friend, Selome who later became our first ever LIA employee, our finance and administration manager, stating clearly she was a long term partner in this ministry. Selome still serves with us to this day.

During the language study period, I began to seek God to know where, and with whom, I was going to initiate the ministry. I first wanted Him to send me to a particular person, an Ethiopian, who would show me where to begin. I confidently expected God to send me a doctor or someone who would help me lay strategies for a medical ministry.

One evening as I prayed, God showed me the figure of a person. I saw it clearly, and registered it in my mind. It was the face of a young college-age man and I started to be on the look out for him.

The very next day as I drove out of the gate, I saw him. He was the watchman at the Baptist General Conference compound where we lived! I talked to him that evening, wanting to know what he knew about medical missions, but all Endashau could tell me was about a children's ministry he was involved in. He had started discipling children in the area and had about twelve children meeting with him once a week. Interestingly, his prayer was that someone would come and help him, and he believed I was the answer to that prayer.

We started working together with these children and asked them to invite their friends. By the end of the month, the group had grown to sixty!

Around that time, we were invited to meet the people who ministered at the Addis Kidan Baptist Church in the Mekanisa slum area. One day Festus and I dropped by on our way home from the language school.

This church, which met in a rented house had only about twenty members. Because it was during the rainy season, everything was muddy and pretty messy, even though it had a cemented floor. We were invited inside and I walked over and stood next to the small wooden pulpit. I heard a clear voice behind me saying I would be back to that church and I would preach from that very pulpit. I quickly turned around, because I thought one of the young men who were showing us around the church was playing a trick on me. To my surprise, there was no one behind me.

I felt very uncomfortable. I did not want to be involved with this community and I did not want to come back to this place, but I knew that was the voice of God and I was to come back! We soon left and I fought hard to forget what God had said.

Not long after this, I found myself in a crisis which made me go back and seek help from that Mekanisa Church in a hurry! I wanted to hold a Christmas Vacation Bible School for the children in our community. So I put up a notice one evening by our gate, asking children to stop by and register.

At six o'clock the next morning, we awoke to the sound of many voices at the gate. When I went out, there were about one thousand children waiting to register. What a shock! After registering four hundred, we had to stop. But despite saying that we could not take any more, about one hundred children waited all day hoping we would consider them.

I had planned for a maximum of one hundred children, but here I was with four hundred and no teachers. I needed help, so I went back to the church. They gave me ten people to help manage the Vacation Bible School and we held it over a three-day period, divided into morning and afternoon shifts.

Prayer is the foundation of any ministry. We are mistaken if we think we do not need it because we are doing "spiritual" things.

During lunch breaks, we took time to pray and intercede for the afternoon meetings. In the evening, we stayed to pray for the next day's morning session. During one of those lunchtime prayer sessions, God spoke again telling me to begin a Bible study at our house with the team that had managed the Vacation Bible School! And so I did.

The Bible study started with eleven people. We used the Alpha materials, which turned out to be very helpful even though they are meant to explain the basics of the gospel to non-Christians. These weekly lessons went on for about four months.

As we came to the end of this Bible study program, we organized another Vacation Bible School, this time with 800 children, after turning away so many. I realized this was not manageable from our home and we moved the ministry to the local church. By then, I had gone back there several times and had spoken from the very pulpit I had despised.

We continued to have Alpha Bible studies in our home and by that summer we had three different groups participating in Alpha on weekly basis. One of my Bible study students took me to the next level in my ministry. She brought a young doctor who was working with Christian Children's Fund and introduced him to us. Dr. Yared had in his own way been praying for God to lead him to a ministry in which to serve. He later became the first National Director of our work in Ethiopia.

These activities and studying of Amharic were going on concurrently. As I came to the end of language school, I began to pray about our medical work in the countryside among the Gumuz. I was going to be flying out there and staying three days a week to establish the work.

Meanwhile, I met two other people who became very significant in the formation of our ministry. Two months before our actual arrival in Ethiopia, I had felt a very strong urge for a prayer partner. God reminded me of Tabitha, my prayer partner in college and He promised to give me another "Tabitha".

On this particular Sunday, we had attended the International Evangelical Church. The person who was supposed to give the sermon that day did not teach; instead, he asked us to turn our chairs around to form small groups. He wanted us to get to know and pray for each other. Two women in my group turned out to be God-sent.

One of them shocked me by how much she looked like my friend Tabitha. She had the same features and the same way of talking. I was even more amazed when I heard her pray because she prayed just like Tabitha used to pray. We became friends and to date, Yenenesh has remained a constant blessing in my life. We meet and pray at least twice a week when I am in Ethiopia. We travel together and fast every Monday while praying for the ministry.

The second woman, Deisalech, who owned a private primary school had gone to school in Kenya, was very friendly. She became a board member for our ministry and has often spoken at our conferences. God is good at making divine connections.

All this happened perfectly as God orchestrated each event in preparation for the next phase of His work.

Chapter 10

The Switch to Urban Poor

What a celebration it was when I graduated from language school! I eagerly had looked forward to this time and the planned subsequent outreach to the Gumuz.

I was, however, in for a surprise. Mission Aviation Fellowship (MAF), which was going to be flying me back and forth to the land of Gumuz lost its registration in Ethiopia. Their flights were therefore grounded so I was not going to have access to the Gumuz after all. I went through a couple of weeks of disillusion and depression.

Meanwhile, the Mekanisa Addis Kidan Church asked me to help them do the required health screening exercise for children who were sponsored by Compassion International through their church. Since I was not busy, I quickly agreed and even got a missionary doctor colleague to help.

We saw about 400 children in three days and filled out their health forms. What we saw was shocking. Over 80% of the children were sick and more than 50% of the sick ones had at least two active diseases. Ironically, most of these illnesses were caused by lack of health education and basic hygiene. We just had to do something in this community. We were hooked again!

I called the church leadership together to share the vision for a health evangelism outreach in this community, beginning with the families of the children we had seen.

We met with the elders in our home to discuss what form such an outreach would take and the resources it would require. It needed to be church-based. We came up with ways to reach the community. I would train a team from the church who would own and implement this ministry.

One of the elders expressed concern, desiring to know if I had ever seen a church do this. Although I had not, I knew we had to do it since not doing it meant disobedience. We had clearly seen a huge need that we could not walk away from. The elder wanted to know what would happen if the ministry failed. My reply was, "We will have obeyed, tried and failed, and so we will have the courage to ask God to instruct us again."

And so we started ministering in this urban slum area, thinking we would work there until the flights to the Gumuz resumed. Meanwhile, I began to get invitations to speak in various churches in Addis Ababa, sharing the Gospel.

I trained the trainers team which had been chosen by the local church. After covering the 80-hour curriculum, we were ready to initiate the program. The curriculum had been put together based on the work with AMREF and among the Maasai, as well as what I had read in Stan Rowland's book .

The first step was to begin a regular time of intercessory prayer and then to have the group call on the parents of the children we had seen to share the findings of the health screening and explain their responsibilities in the health of their children. They were to explain the causes of these diseases and how it was not good to treat them, only to let them fall back into the same situation again.

Fortunately, the families were eager to work with the church to improve their community. They selected a church-community committee with nine members. We developed a training curriculum for the committee and they readily completed the training and graduated. By graduation time, two of the committee members had committed their lives to Christ. Meanwhile, we continued to pray and work.

The next step was to choose one health agent for every 10 homes we were targeting. This was in addition to the other Christian health agents chosen by the church. All these were to work as change agents in both spiritual and health issues. Once their training had commenced, they began to visit the homes they had been assigned.

Our work in the community was aimed at bringing health knowledge to the homes, with the desire to change attitudes and practices to improve people's health.

God was with us. This was the only intervention that was undertaken in the community, and six months later when we did the second health screening we saw a big reduction in disease rates. We were encouraged. At the same time, many decisions were being made for Christ during the home visits and baptisms were increasing in the church.

The church mobilized the community into health ventures such as clearing trash, cleaning and repairing public toilets, and helping the sick and elderly by visiting, cleaning and repairing their homes.

We showed the Jesus film on several occasions and the response was remarkable. We divided the community into clusters of 40 families each, and began to focus on seeing where there was a need to change behavior patterns. We would then mobilize the people to do something about their own needs.

Following a needs assessment survey, we realized that several families were fully dependent on begging for their livelihood. To assist them we started a church fund and began a revolving loan system to help these families generate income.

By the end of the first year, we had over 100 members in the church, five times the starting number. This did not include those who attended but had not become members. This urban community was now organized into working groups with the ground work laid for viable intervention when such a need arose.

Around that time, God spoke to us again. He was going to grow the ministry. A little trickle would come together to form a huge flow.

God opened other doors to improve the health and economic status of the community:

- The revolving fund became a full-fledged micro-enterprise.

- Toilet construction work was started.

- A vocational training school began, teaching dressmaking and carpentry.

- More organizations were attracted by the change and wanted to help also.

- A kindergarten was established.

- Child sponsorship program was initiated.

This was all very encouraging and it was supported with prayer and fasting on a regular basis.

Below is an excerpt from our year report highlighting what we accomplished in the six months after I finished language school:

- *Alpha discipleship classes are being handed over to the Addis Kidan community church and four teachers have been trained.*

- *The December VBS went very well. The Addis Kidan church is planning the upcoming April VBS on their own.*

- *The last budget was 80% met by the church and they were responsible for all the teaching.*

- *Ninety new children joined the Saturday church school program.*

- *The church leaders have accepted the vision for community health evangelism.*

- *Eight trainers graduated and are able to train and manage the project.*

- *A community committee of nine members was set up and trained.*

- *Forty graduated health agents are doing community mobilization activities and home-visits.*

- *A revolving fund has been set up through the church and benefits 14 families who previously lived on begging.*

All the objectives of the first phase of the health project have been satisfactorily completed. The second phase will be a three-year program mainly run by the church. Community vocational training, health training and teaching centers will be set up along with a water and sanitation project and house renovation activities.

Two other churches, similar to Mekanisa Addis Kidan, are ready to begin community health projects. The two salaried members of the training team will be sent to these churches to facilitate the projects.

With the trained team in Addis Ababa, when the time comes for the Gumuz work to start, things will be simpler.

And they were simpler! These two trainers ended up being the ones who a year later went to the Gumuz to carry out the first training of trainers and help start the community health evangelism work there, linking the program among the Gumuz with the local clinic and the church under the resident CMF missionary. This was the very place Festus and I had visited and seen the mountain God had shown to us as a sign confirming our timing to go to Ethiopia.

Before replicating the Pilot Project, we felt the need to do a joint evaluation of the work with outside evaluators. They worked with our team and joint evaluation was provided. These gave a very good report, describing our work as an effective strategy to alleviate poverty and also as a tool for evangelism. Part of their report read:

Poverty eradication has been on the agenda of the global community for many decades. However, the dream of getting rid of poverty has not been modeled in such an effective way. The search for alternative approaches that are effective continues, and this is a model worthy of emulation.

The concern of the church in dealing with this problem can be traced back to the early establishment of the church, and even during the Old Testament times. God's call and concern for the poor is evident throughout the Bible, being the responsibility of God's people.

Peoples' needs are both physical and spiritual, and that can hamper healthy human development. Ethiopian needs are diverse, being physical and spiritual. Many die because of different beliefs and taboos that discourage seeking medical treatment.

Therefore, wholistic ministry is essential to meet the physical as well as spiritual needs of our people. This evaluation has confirmed the effect of wholistic ministry and its relevance to this poor community. The process of evaluation has confirmed the impact of the program, which was mainly due to attitude change. This came out through discussions, interviews, observation and home visits.

We realized the work was expanding fast and a system was necessary to manage it. We therefore began to do the groundwork to establish a local non-governmental organization, Life in Abundance (LIA), to own and manage the expansion of this work. On this we reported in our newsletter:

This is a local association in the making, which Florence is facilitating. It has a board of seven members, mainly health professionals. Once registered, LIA will work with evangelical churches to raise awareness of the need for wholistic ministry, and help implement this work through national churches.

Florence sees LIA as the vehicle for wholistic programs in this country and beyond. Using the current community project as a pilot, we hope to disseminate the strategy to several other churches.

God continued to be very faithful. Partnerships began to develop and the ministry continued to grow. In our next report in September 2000, we wrote:

> *The pilot wholistic ministry project has become a model of integrated ministry for other churches. Six Addis Ababa churches have visited and studied the work, and will be setting up projects. Friends from the Catholic Church and one other evangelical church are also starting similar ministries, using LIA's model.*
>
> *LIA has taken off, is well funded, and will be facilitating the work with these new sites. LIA has also started training other Christian organizations, empowering them for wholistic ministry. A staff team from Food for the Hungry Ethiopia is one of the organization teams we have trained in the ten day training. They will be a resource for any agency that wants to set up similar programs.*
>
> *A vocational training center in the pilot church project has been established. Twenty women are in the third month of seamstress training. Carpentry work will begin in September. The machinery for carpentry is in place now.*
>
> *The ministry's impact is high with regard to poverty issues, health education and evangelism.*
>
> *Two new church community health ministries have been set up. One of these is a pilot project for Debre Birhan, a town in northern Ethiopia. Twenty-two new trainers have been trained and have in turn trained two new community committees and 70 agents. Both projects are at the end of their first phase.*

We continued to be available to teach and disciple as time allowed, but we limited our engagements to Addis Ababa, although we did some conferences outside of Addis. We also hosted summer interns from the USA.

Our two boys at this time were in third grade and kindergarten. Festus continued to do the field administration work for our mission agency. We enjoyed a nine-day visit to Kenya, meeting family and our accountability partners. My brother Simon was at this time a Pastor in Kenya. He and his wife also visited us in Ethiopia. Simon is gifted in prophecy and we wanted to tap into this gift to set up intercessory teams for our ministries, to empower the local churches in this area. He came with a colleague and their ministry in Addis Ababa was well received and very effective. They were able to minister in many churches.

Chapter 11

An Organization is Born

All this may look like clock work. It may seem like we had it all easy. We had our difficult times, though. Writing from Ethiopia at the end of our second year, these were our feelings:

> *What makes the life we lead now in Ethiopia as missionaries so difficult? We had a choice, yet we chose this out of other available options, by faith believing God called us to serve Him. This is the hardest part - living out that faith on a daily basis, believing that He who called us is faithful, that though we do not see Him, He is guiding and directing. We are holding on when we have no reason to, and trusting that the Lord will give us the next instructions.*

> *As for the children, they had no choice in our commitment to serve God here and even when we see their skin spotted from continuous fleabites we still agree with God that we are where He wants us to be. That takes faith.*

> *No one ever said it would be easy. Christ did not call us to comfort and ease. It is all about going and following Him. But He does keep His promise. Yes! – He remains with us always, to the very end of the earth.*

> *The Lord calls each one of us Christians to count the cost before walking this journey of faith, yet He supplies our needs. It is costly, tiring and inconvenient in many ways, and there are easier choices.*

> *Living for Christ is hard – whether in the mission field or right in our comfort zone but take courage. Be faithful and fully committed*

to what the Lord has entrusted to you. Hang in there – Christ's grace is sufficient and there will be seasons of refreshing.

Just before this, we had written in another newsletter:

The open doors and opportunities for ministry have put us in an advantageous position to take the gospel to the homes of very needy people as we address their needs. It is, however, neither easy nor convenient. We serve in what is now ranked the poorest country in the world. Sometimes we feel the attacks of the evil one hitting us. Nevertheless, we know we cannot stop. The work has to be done, as thousands are waiting hopefully. God renews our strength and the joy He gives is sweet.

Pray with us as we press on. We want to see God's Kingdom come to the communities we are working with. Has the Ethiopia-Eritrea war negatively affected us? No. It has made us realize the work has to move faster, that lives must be saved. There is no better place right now to be than in this country, for the fields are RIPE! The need has especially worsened with the war, as community financial resources have been redirected.

⟞⟋⟍⟝

Living for Christ is hard – whether in the mission field or at home in our comfort zone. Let us be faithful and fully committed to what the Lord has entrusted to us.

⟞⟋⟍⟝

The third year was actually the most difficult and decisive in our ministry. Through yet another divine intervention, I met a Norwegian doctor who became a ministry partner. When he visited our work, I mentioned the *Community Health Evangelism* book by Stan Rowland that I had come across in Nairobi.

I had assumed Stan was no longer alive, that this was a work done a long time ago. But my Norwegian friend knew and had worked with Stan! In fact, Stan was then going to be giving training in Yemen in just a few weeks! I immediately decided I needed to be at that conference and my Norwegian friend offered to pay my ticket. I gladly accepted his offer.

I celebrated my 40th birthday in Yemen and met Stan, the man who had obeyed God and put the community health evangelism strategy on paper, making it available to many who never met him. Since then, we have partnered with his organization, Life Wind, to expand wholistic ministry in Africa, and I began to attend conferences and to meet with other people involved in our kind of ministry.

Now it became obvious that God was establishing an international ministry. The groundwork in Ethiopia was good. We had a strong board of seven Ethiopian nationals heading Life in Abundance Ethiopia. Meanwhile I began to take a backseat role to allow the work to take form, as I began to establish the international chapter of the ministry.

An international board was formed, comprising two Americans, a Swiss, a Congolese pastor, a Liberian missionary, a Sudanese nutrition specialist, three Ethiopian doctors, a seminary lecturer and myself. God brought this group of people with different training together in order that many parts of Africa might experience wholistic healing and redemption.

As a family, we began to feel led to take a course we had not anticipated in order to achieve what God was molding our ministry to be. It was time to leave the CMF team in Ethiopia and concentrate on this wholistic ministry in a focused way. But the CMF board asked us to continue the ministry still under CMF.

In order for the work to continue effectively, a CMF Ethiopia urban team was formed to work with the urban poor. The urban poor department was also created in the CMF head office. The work had good backing from the Indianapolis office and this enhanced our confidence.

Festus felt he needed training in missions to strengthen our impact in the local churches. He applied and was admitted to Fuller Theological Seminary and was in the field on and off. Meanwhile, we also began to explore new areas. We were invited to Khartoum to explore ministry opportunities there.

The situation there was even worse than what we had seen in Ethiopia. Sharing of my experience after the visit, I noted:

> *I stood on a heap of mud, caused by recent rains in the capital of Sudan. Gazing through the displaced peoples' camp that stretched to the horizon, I got confused.*
>
> *My facial expression must have revealed it. A leader of one of the main denominations in Sudan who stood by my side put his hand on my shoulder and began to talk, softly at first, and then more confidently as confidence was regained.*
>
> *"Florence," he said, "see the opportunity. God brought these people from the south where they practiced idolatry. Culture and ungodly traditional practices bound them. They have been displaced from comfort zones and are now open to evangelization. Do not just see the misery. See how to minister to their physical needs and use it as a channel for what is eternal. God has brought them to where we can reach them. He now holds us accountable to do the job."*
>
> *I cried a lot during that visit to Sudan. The urban poor are receptive and to be found in all cities and towns in Africa. Our city of Addis Ababa, Ethiopia, is no exception. The urban poor are available for integrated ministry. We see Christ in their faces saying, "I am hungry, thirsty, a stranger, naked, sick, in prison. Will you do something?"*

Invited by the Kenya CMF team, my prayer partner and I briefly went to train church leaders and clinic workers from the Maasai churches on the wholistic ministry outreach. Fifty-three trainers were trained from ten local churches. The leaders from the clinics we had worked with, as well as leaders from the local churches were there. What a great time of reunion and fellowship! We worshipped in tears, gratefully acknowledging what God had done.

By 2002, we were ready for a break. This would also be a time to evaluate how the system worked without us. We spent nine months with partners in the US as Festus continued with his studies at Fuller.

Living in Pasadena as a family turned out to be yet another time of ministry growth for us. Partnerships were expanded. Led by the Lord, we incorporated Life in Abundance as a 501(c)3 non-profit organization in California. Two other Americans joined the existing LIA International board and I was appointed president for LIA International.

While in the United States, we raised funds for a new addition to our ministry. We were thinking of taking on a street children's program in Debre Birhan, north of Addis Ababa. This was to be a family based rehabilitation program for street children. A total of three hundred and twenty children were targeted, and two of the local churches we partnered with would be involved in the work. This program has been a wonderful pilot project for wholistic work among street children. We have now replicated this in Addis Ababa, in Jimma and in two other places in Kenya, where we are targeting the same number of children.

The strategy is to work with the families, or the foster families of the children on the streets, to create a stable child and home within three years. Emotional, physical, social and spiritual interventions are carried out, enabling disintegrated families to bond, heal and begin anew. Both rehabilitative and preventive components for the vulnerable are implemented. This is a great and cost effeective option to orphanages or international adoptions commonly addressed through our 'They Matter' campaigns.

God continued to open forums where we could share the vision with other leaders. We began to be involved in regional and international conferences, National Missionary Conventions and MedSend International. We had a chance to visit and ignite the vision in other 'restricted' countries in Africa. Some of the new forums that were now opened to us included the Christian Medical and Dental Association, the Global Missions Health Conference and MedSend International.

We were also pleased to see that the work in Ethiopia, in fact, did continue well in our absence. Through LIA, effective systems were put in place and the trained workers in each of the project sites continued to carry out the wholistic ministry activities with no interruptions.

Chapter 12

Danger Signs Along the Way

I know no more geater danger sign than compromise. Compromise is opting for an ungodly way to do what God has asked of us, and it is a tool of the devil that really appeals to his victims.

I confronted this when we were just about to leave for the mission field. With the UN offer for a job in Botswana, I began to seriously consider taking it and doing missions indirectly. Rather than going where God had called me to go I thought I could send the much-needed resource, money. But I am thankful God let me know it was me He needed, not my money.

Having been in the field for some time now, I realize how true that is. God has plenty of money for His work. What He needs are people to use it in His work. There is no vision from God that lacks provision. Some people have realized this and have tried to come up with flesh-birthed visions so they can exploit God's rich resources.

Compromise, or wishing for a more convenient way, has been a serious enemy of the Kingdom. Sometimes we try to 'cut' parts of the cross or try to make the way of the cross more comfortable. And we could distort it to the point where it no longer looks anything like what it was meant to be. Remember, God is calling to full obedience, not compromise.

Another challenge we tend to also come up against is delay. I will do it, of course, I will just do it later. I can only imagine the many opportunities of service that I have missed through the years because I did not respond to the prompting of the Holy Spirit.

One day, when I was speaking to a certain group, I felt a very strong prompting from God to pray publicly for the healing of someone with a lesion, probably cancer, on his or her leg. I saw a mental picture of the wound and I felt a very strong urge to stop teaching and pray just then for that person but I decided I would wait and pray at the closing of the meeting time.

As I continued teaching, I scanned my audience to see if any of them looked sick. They looked happy and no signs of pain were evident on any face. So I decided it would be an embarrassment to pray for someone with a wound when the person was not in the meeting. I opted to pray later that evening.

Beware of: Compromise – Delay – Prayerlessness – Dependence on own resources

When the session ended, I left feeling very encouraged and greatly used of God. However, just as I drove out of the gate, there she was, walking home, a smiling woman from the audience who was wearing a white shawl over her knee length dress. For some reason, I looked down from the smiling face to her legs and I saw the same picture I had seen as I taught. She had a sore at that exact location and I had missed the opportunity to obey God and minister to her through prayer! Just then, the car behind me honked to let me know I was blocking the exit.

Since that time, at the risk of being embarrassed or acting like a fool, I have committed myself to obeying God's prompting. I have been wrong at times, but for the sake of the times when I am right, I will stick to this principle. The pain of that awful mistake keeps me in check.

Prayerlessness is another danger for people in the ministry. We tend to think we do not need prayer because we are engaged in 'spiritual' things. How wrong we are! It is an irony to be involved in God's work without constantly seeking His guidance. He has the blueprint, yet we go about guessing or trying to figure out what it is He wants us to do for Him.

At Life in Abundance, we have known how dependent we ought to be on prayer from the beginning. We have chosen prayer as our ministry strategy. It is the lifeline of our ministry. We have an overnight prayer session once a month. Monday is our day of prayer and fasting and we also meet on Tuesday evenings with key players to pray for the different interventions. Whenever we encounter a 'roadblock', we pray. When we do not know what to do, we pray. Prayer to us is never enough.

Choose prayer as a ministry strategy.

I have very often fought the desire and urge to do things the way I know how, leaning on my own understanding. I realize that God may use the knowledge He has graciously given us, but sometimes He desires to use other ways that will ensure that the glory goes back to him. He is so creative in the way He does things, which brings adventure to His service. Sometimes it calls for blind faith. I have sensed this a few times when I am speaking a word of knowledge to a group, letting my tongue go loose!

It is the same with projects. I have seen God begin in some ways I never would and follow Him in steps that keep me focused on Him because I have not been that way before, all the while trusting He knows what He is doing. Usually, we come through to the end of the project in an easier and more kingdom-enriching manner.

I have to keep reminding myself that I must decrease so that He [the Lord] may increase. I am to take the passenger's seat and let Him drive. It does not mean I do not participate, but I totally relinquish control. Of course, with my kind of personality, I have had to keep constraining myself into submission to God's leading.

Sometimes God calls us to things we cannot easily explain to family members, some of whom we are alienated to socially. At such times, there is an inclination to explain so that they may understand and give us their blessing. Sometimes they may understand yet at other times they may come out strongly against what we are doing or intend to do. Some of our loved ones, meaning well, but not understanding fully God's call on us, can actually lead us astray.

We should not make excuses to disobey God, but we need to be wise in following and sharing with others things concerning our walk with God. There are things that are best kept to ourselves to keep us out of trouble. Joseph told his dreams to his brothers and that got him into much trouble and cost his father many years of unnecessary sorrow. Mary, on the other hand, kept to herself the things the angel told her and saw God rescue her marriage and spare her the shame she would have undergone.

In whatever ministry God has called us to, we will meet people who will think we are being overly pious or self-centered as we pursue God's will for our life. Some will want us to explain in advance how you will survive, let alone accomplish what you set out to do. And many times we will lack words to explain or to defend our position.

Think of Abraham, taking his son Isaac up that mountain to sacrifice him. The son whom he had waited for so long! How do you explain it? How can one even utter the words God had said? Think of Moses telling the Children of Israel to march forward when the Red Sea is right before them. March into the sea? And how was He planning to keep them fed in the desert? What about water? How do you explain the possibility of the success of such a project?

God does not tell us to do something because it is reasonable or well planned or with foreseeable outcome. He calls us to trust Him and go about doing His work by faith. In fact without faith it is impossible to please God.

It is logical to put our efforts into what will cause us to be appreciated and admired, and sometimes when we do what God wants us to do this is the result. But there are also times when we have to go against what the world expects of us, and this becomes even more difficult if those making the demands are donors or supporters who have control over what we do in terms of providing resources. It becomes costly when we choose against their wishes.

God does not give us an option in this area. His way is what He asks you to do. When conflict of interest arises, let God's word guide you in making the decision. It is adequate if we choose to obey His guidance.

> *All scripture is God breathed and is useful for teaching, rebuking, correcting and training in righteousness, so that the man of God may be thoroughly equipped for every good work.*
>
> *— 2 Timothy 3: 16-17*

In Paul's first letter to Timothy, the Bible warns the young not to let the world despise them because they are young. There are many things that could be despised, not just age. And youth, as the word is used in the context, could represent gender, old age, status, physical appearance, ethnicity, language, or whatever is in you that people can despise. If God has chosen to use you, trust in His ability to help you make a good choice.

Whatever you do, do not think of it as insignificant no matter how small. Do not let anyone despise your small beginnings. God is in the building program, starting with small things. Do not let your starting capital stop you from beginning. Let it be a seed for what God will do.

Whatever challenges you face, I encourage you with the word Paul told Timothy:

> *Timothy, guard what has been entrusted to your care. Turn away from godless chatter and opposing ideas of what is falsely called knowledge, which some have professed and in so doing have wandered from the faith. Grace be with you.*
>
> *— 1 Timothy 6:20-21*

Chapter 13

Joy on the Mountain

Not all of us get to experience the thrill of success, since not all of us are willing to take risks. The person who risks nothing has nothing to gain. He or she may avoid failure and much suffering, but at the same time, they will never enjoy the thrill of achievement. I have realized I would be better off dead if each passing day does not find me pressing on to achieve that which the Lord has called me to do.

There is fulfillment in knowing we are obeying His will. We will never have complete joy if we do not heed His call; instead, we will be fleeing like Jonah with no rest and no peace. Whatever mountain God has called you to climb, you will be more joyful climbing it than feasting at a king's house.

Another thing that makes this a joyful venture is the company you get. The sweet ongoing communion with Jesus! And this is not once in a while but always. The Lord Jesus accompanies us as we walk His path. I have known what it feels like to deviate from that path. It leads to having His presence depart, and nothing can replace it.

Walking with the Lord takes us on an adventure. Wow! The adventure of life, with the assurance that we will be victorious. It may not be success as the world would gauge it. It is success in Kingdom terms and in eternal things.

Usually the Lord does not give the full map, although He may give a snap preview of a something to come. We see the map in retrospect as it falls open behind us. Things unfold by the day. Thus, each new turn becomes a joyful adventure as our trusted and faithful Guide leads us on.

The path the Lord leads us through may be dangerous at times, sharply ascending or descending or with very dark valleys. Sometimes you may experience loss, other times rest and feasting, but all the time tightly supported by his hand.

There are bridges that lead to fearful territories, risking our very lives! These bridges represent the temptation to turn back and continue on familiar ground. But such bridges are best burned as soon as we cross, leaving the way forward as our only choice!

In the meantime, God may allow some small peaks of joy as He shows you the fruit of your labour. During our fifth year of ministry in Ethiopia, we sent this letter to our partners:

The phone rang at 10:00 pm on a Friday night. Who could be calling so late? It was from the Mekanisa Church where we started our ministry nearly four years ago. The evangelist was speaking with unusual calmness. Knowing the life and motivation this man generates, I could tell right away something was up!

In the next thirty minutes, he narrated with great humility and tears the amazing happenings in his community. Going back to the start of our ministry, he declared that the harvest time had come! I was invited the next day to witness the baptism of twenty young men from the garbage dump, part of the target community for this church.

Only a week previously the church had baptized forty two people from the Leprosy village, also a part of the target community. We had been making home visits to the lepers and constructing houses for them.

Six months earlier, we had pleaded with an organization not to cancel a project aimed at repairing two hundred mud houses for leper families. At the cost of tears (they are common) and a change of organizational policy, the project was allowed and has changed lives!

What a strong witness for the church this house construction was! The lepers experienced God's love, so how could they not respond? The neighbors saw this and requested teaching from the Word of God. Now, a church has been born and nine more cell churches meet every Sunday evening! The Mekanisa church is packed on Sundays. Left and right, people are making commitments for Christ.

And the gospel moves on. We have started a similar ministry with three sister churches and the Mekanisa Addis Kidan Church has released money for seed projects from our CMF funding, to be directed to the new churches.

Through our local partner organization, we are reaching a dozen communities through Community Health Evangelism, which meets people's needs and allows God to do the rest as the Word is proclaimed.

Is it worth it?

People keep saying how hard it must be for us now to be separated as a family. Festus is in California finalizing his studies at Fuller. This will be necessary in the church here because of the need for continued Christian teaching in the ministry. Florence and the boys must remain in the field. It may be hard, but with the results we are seeing we could still do it even if it was twice as hard.

What next? We have signed agreements with the Ethiopian government to do two family-based street children projects! One has been running for a year, targeting three hundred children. The other one kicks off next week and this week we identified a project donor. Again, three hundred children will be reached.

With the hunger situation in Ethiopia, God is enabling us to respond. Of the two hundred and fifty children enrolled and three hundred families registered with our project, half are already being reached and we are trusting God for provision so that none will die. We hope to sustain them until June when the rains come.

During the spring break, Florence will be in our neighboring country, Sudan. We pray that the ministry in Ethiopia will be replicated there and beyond. Our prayer is for dozens of countries in Africa to be reached through this ministry.

Sometimes these victories come after scaling discouraging and dangerous rocks, which may cost lives! In another update, we wrote:

We have a ministry team in the north, six hours' drive from Addis Ababa where they are ministering to a very poor community. The level of poverty is depressing physically, but they are spiritually 'hungry' too. They have suffered from the recent drought.

These team members are part of a poor local evangelical church, which has about thirty members. Through them, we have implemented small-scale projects, targeting destitute families, children and the government prison. For about two years now, the team has been persecuted by the Orthodox Church which is very strong in this area.

Recently our team was very sad because we had just lost one of the ministry team members to an inoperable brain tumor which came about suddenly and had him in coma for two weeks. Several Orthodox Church members who knew him from his work with the poor came for his funeral but this displeased the Orthodox priests and those who attended the funeral were shunned by their church.

A hot crisis discussion meeting followed. At the end of the session, the community completely supported the evangelical church, recognizing how they have been mindful of the destitute and have shown what love is all about. They praised the construction of the prison toilet. Close to 100 people decided they had found reason and courage to join the small church.

The next day was Sunday and the little church was so packed that they had to meet outside the church building. There were several baptisms that day. This only happened two weeks ago and a great revival has set in. We are very excited that God has put an end to the persecution and caused the little acts of love to turn into big doors for His glory. We praise God that the church has gained popularity and we look forward to a time of growth and major harvest.

Whatever we confront along the way, we are reminded that God's work continues. We realize that we harvest where others have planted. We must continue to sow the seed that others may also share in the joy of harvesting, someday.

For us, the greatrest joy has been seeing what God so clearly showed in the past being fulfilled. In the recent drought in Ethiopia, we were able to respond to the hunger situation through our partner churches, thus averting starvation for many.

The lives of the poor have been affected and in some cases radically changed because we chose to obey God. We are aware that poverty will not be eradicated until Jesus comes. But our aim is to have the converting glory of God come into whatever area we occupy, changing communities, one person at a time: one sick person being healed; a hungry one being fed; a child enabled to go to school; one sinner repents; one woman is trained in dressmaking; another learns how to prevent illness through basic hygiene; a leper gets a roof over her house; other resources are properly directed to meet needs.

The smiling faces tell it all. Our aim is a smile from the heart as we continually innovate and come up with new ways of doing things so that self-sufficiency is achieved and sustained. We are constantly involving the people we minister to in identifying how best to serve them.

We aim at meeting both physical and spiritual needs. Knowing the importance of meeting physical needs, and yet bearing eternity in mind and the value of the soul, we seek for ways to address physical and spiritual needs together.

These are but glimpses of what God is doing and we eagerly await to see more, and we know what the end result will be. The nations will be gathered to Him. Oh, we will sing! When the new heaven and new earth are ushered in and the new Jerusalem comes down, then God will dwell among us. He will wipe every tear from the eyes of His beloved. He will live with us.

Chapter 14

What Next?

I have had several opportunities to travel and ministry in different parts of the world. Such opportunities have increased in the recent years, especially since my travel to the USA. Meetings with our partners have also been part of this travel.

I was in prayer preparing for one of those visits that was to take me through Philadelphia, Pennsylvania, when God spoke to me in what seemed a weird picture of two women and a dog and a word – prayer partner. I shared that with my family and since we couldn't make meaning of it, we put it aside.

It wasn't until I was on that trip that the meaning became clear. When I arrived for one of the meetings of a Christian foundation in Pennsylvania, the woman director I was supposed to meet was out of the office for an errand. I decided to wait and made myself comfortable with my laptop in the waiting room.

After a little while, a woman walked in and inquired if I was waiting for Nancy. Having confirmed that, she introduced herself as Barbara, a prayer partner of Nancy. She invited me to accompany her on a few errands, the last of which would be to pick up Nancy and head back to the office.

When we got into the car, I noticed she had a dog. That is when my mind went back to the vision I had seen. I noticed the dog and Barbara were the exact replica of what I had earlier been shown by God. Then the prayer partner part of the vision clicked, but I was to wait and see if Nancy would be as I had seen her in the vision. When she eventually turned up, what God had shown was confirmed. She was the very person I had been shown.

Now, the big question was: why did God show me this? All I could tell was that this was no ordinary appointment. In fact, my earlier attempts to plan the exit flight from Pennsylvania had been hindered and God had spoken to me to leave that open.

Little did I know that we would quickly get acquainted with these two women and their dog and head out to their home at the Eastern shore for the weekend, and much more.

I was not surprised when, a few months later, God confirmed that our next base when in the USA for the following two years would not be any of the wonderful and logical choices that we had, but Pennsylvania, in the same neighborhood with these two women. They became as a family, daily connecting with us and praying together – sometimes for hours on the phone.

This made me realize that God is still in the business of guiding His people. I have come to a level where at each airport I ask for sneak previews. It has been fun, as surrender to God deepens.

I will instruct you and teach you in the way you should go; I will counsel you and watch over you.

— *Psalms 32:8*

I have had two dreams of what I wanted to be when I grow up. One was to be an ambassador. I grew up thinking I wanted to be appointed as the Kenyan Ambassador to Switzerland. I still think that is a place I would want to live…when I grow old.

The second dream is that I would be an advocate to represent the needs of women and children in powerful forums such as the UN.

Recently, God showed me that I had achieved both of these. Actually, I have achieved much more than I ever imagined in both dreams.

I have been to Switzerland and I have spoken in forums in Geneva and Zurich, not as the Kenyan ambassador, but as an ambassador of the Kingdom of God. I have represented my homeland in several forums and I go to these nations as a dignitary because God has thus ordained it.

> *But you are a chosen people, a royal priesthood, a holy nation, a*
> *people belonging to God, that you may declare the praises of Him*
> *who called you out of darkness into His wonderful light.*
> — *1 Peter 2: 9*

The other achievement is in the area of advocacy. I continuously advocate for women and children at the highest level — the throne of God. I have complete access to it and I am guaranteed of God's ear from wherever I am, at any time, and for every need. I am backed by resources, both in the physical and in the spiritual realm that cause an impact and have eternal results. There is no earthly power that can replicate this!

The work God wanted me to do in Ethiopia came to a suceccess-ful completion when a national team, with a national board became functional. Then three years later, Sudan and Kenya also acquired their national teams. This was followed by four other countries. Today, as we start the Fall of 2008, we have teams and national boards in seven countries in Africa, and over seventy LIA full time staff.

The last two years have found our family extending our stay in the USA. Festus is finalizing his doctorate in missions at the Palmer Theological Seminary' at Eastern University. During these two years, I have had a good chance to focus on the LIA USA office in Pasadena. That too has come of age with a board, systems of accountability and a capable team of USA nationals as staff.

Another transition? Just this summer, seeking for a sign again, God has clearly confirmed my role in the next chapter. As I continue to work with the international board which has representatives from all our national boards, I will continue to work alongside our national team leaders. I will also continue to facilitate new initiatives in the existing as well as new ministry fields.

Meanwhile, God has contined working in other ways. Our boys are growing. Jay just turned eighteen and is now a freshman at Eastern University in Pennsylvania. Kyalo is in eighth grade, boarding at Rift Valley Academy, Kijabe, Kenya.

One of my long term desires also recently came to fulfillment. I was ordained as a minister of the gospel. What a moment to publicly declare my full surrender to God's call and know I am in this to the end. I was branded and totally enlisted in His service. It feels like the show is just starting.

In this transition and new status, I got a new conviction. Recently while attending our son's track event, I went deep into reflection. I could tell God was about to speak to me.

I realized I could provide for my physical, spiritual and other basic needs pretty well, especially if I tried hard enough and positioned myself right. Even if I failed, it would be because of unavoidable circumstances like acts of nature or disease.

Then it occurred to me that taking advantage of some things might be in direct conflict with God's will for me. His call may lead me to risky situations, bring me to precarious moments, take me to lonely places and expose me to conditions where my needs are far from met. I realized it was time to take another step. It hit me again: discipleship. Nothing short of that! Being His must rise above my needs even though so legitimate. In many cases, they align. And that is usually wonderful. But in those few cases where they will not, a defining choice is made. Sacrifice of the desired. His hands speak of sacrifice, other than what he would have desired. Surrender to His Father's will. To be His. That's when the cost comes home.

Soon afterwards the decision was put to the test. I was to leave the USA where my family was temporarily based to visit one of our operation bases in Africa, in a rather unsafe area. The closer I came to the time of departure, the clearer it became to me that this was the final trip. I would not survive it and yet I was to still go. It became so clear during the final days of packing that I chose to copy legal and travel documents and leave them where my husband could quickly get to them.

I left the Philadelphia airport then transited through Detroit to Amsterdam. By the time I arrived in Amsterdam, I was completely broken and willing to lay down my life. I even began to sense the next connecting flight may be the end, and concluded that I needed to call the team I was visiting to let them know that even if I did not make it, the mission was vital and they should proceed.

In Amsterdam, I went upstairs to the lounge bathrooms. Being such an early hour, I thought I could spend some time in those bathrooms alone, pouring my heart to God and getting set to head Home.

But when I got to the bathrooms, I was disappointed to find a woman in there, brushing her hair. As I entered, she was equally surprised because she stopped brushing her hair and uncomfortably stared at me. I mumbled a greeting and went into the bathroom. I came out a few moments later to find that she had put away her bag and was standing, waiting for me. She then asked me if I was a medical doctor. I wondered where we had met and looked at her closely. Then she asked the second question, wanting to know if I was a minister of the gospel. I confirmed I was both, only to have her get so excited and begin to pour out her reason for being in that very bathroom.

She had been in prayer for me that whole week. She serves in a church in Washington DC and had been on a mission with the UN to Tanzania. God had impressed on her to pray for me and she was to come meet me in that bathroom to pray with me.

The rest of our time was out of this world. We prayed together and she told me several other prophetic messages. She then said I was not to fear for though I thought this mission was unto death, that was not the case. That I would be returning through Amsterdam since my work is not yet over. She gave me her business card and ran off to catch her connecting flight.

I did come back though Amsterdam a week later, and I did stop at that very bathroom to thank God for His faithfulness. As a matter of fact, I always make it a point, every time I pass through here on my way to or from the USA, to go to that bathroom and thank God, who has me alive for a purpose.

If that woman hadn't given me her business card, I probably would have thought I met an angel. She is real. By profession, she is a professor in pediatrics and an associate pastor serving in a church on the East coast of the US.

Chapter 15

The Emerging Strategy in Missions

The following is a presentation I made at the Global Missions Health Conference in Louisville, Kentucky, November 2006. It is available in CD format and can be requested at www.liaint.org.

There was a time when a medical professional would move to a third world country somewhere like in Africa, would learn the local language and then would engage in something like curative medicine as ministry to the unreached. A cross cultural missionary providing service to make a difference.

Today, that strategy is behind us. God has given us a new strategy to embrace His agenda in missions today. Reflecting on the picture I grew up with of cross cultural missionaries, then what I had in mind as I went into missions, followed by the reality of my twelve years walk on that path, I share a testimony of the emerging strategy in missions to the developing nations. I relate this to the first hand opportunities I have had to interact with ministries in Asia, Central America, the Middle East and Africa.

Introduction

In Africa, the word of testimony is well appreciated. We love to testify of what God has done. God is currently revealing himself to me in a new dimension. Faithful has taken on a new meaning for me. You think you know God until yet again He shows up in a new aspect. He is so faithful. Incomparable. Deeply faithful. I praise His name.

My prayer over this Global Missions' gathering this weekend is that there will be a canopy of God's presence and a glow of the Spirit of God. May these next days be a refreshment in His shade. May He come through as faithful to you. I pray that our sharing tonight will be worship to Him. To His glory.

I want to share what I have seen about emerging missions' strategy in developing nations. I am no authority to draw any conclusions, other than bring a report of what is happening. I testify to this with biases so I submit these to the Spirit of God.

I was brought up in East Africa, in a Kenyan rural village setting. I grew up knowing of a mission sending agency that had missionaries in that part of the world.

One missionary and his family lived pretty close to us. He knew the local language well enough to communicate. On special days he would do a devotion at our elementary school. He would visit a few prominent leaders in the community, and share tea or even the local food. Not many people went over to his house unless they had a reason or special need. Most of the requests people would come with were for financial support or medical help. He worked with the local church, and would do a sermon every other Sunday. He would also teach the baptism classes and baptize new believers.

During his stay, he constructed a church building transforming it from what I am told was a local mud and wood structure to a solid concrete building. Sometimes he had teams from his home church come help build the church, but the nationals were not involved. Most of the building materials came from the main town.

He left when I was in high school because his children needed college education back home. He is remembered to this day for his attempt to talk the language, his building skills and his white truck that got stuck in the mud every so often and the community members helped pull it out. I remember his children who were a bit older than me. They came to children's church and played with us.

When he left, the national minister took over the work. He did not need the missionary house and could not afford to keep the electric generator going. So several years later that house was converted to a guest house of some sort. Over time, the congregation grew and they constructed another brick church building that could accommodate more people, demolishing the stone church building. The church bell still hangs from a tree by the church, but it is no longer used.

The same mission agency had another missionary. She was a single middle aged woman, a teacher by training, serving as the principal to a boarding girls' high school that was set up by the mission and served our district. Two of my sisters went to this school. She had a red bicycle and would often be seen riding to the shops and post office. She also came to the church on Sundays accompanying the students for the service.

During her term of stay, she supervised the construction of the school and established the school management system. She died suddenly from a road traffic accident and is buried in the school she established. After she died, the school experienced several setbacks, mainly financial and was eventually taken over by a local association. It still runs, makes some profit , but it is not run as a Christian school.

There was also a mission health center not far from us that was very well known for the services it provided, which were outstanding compared to the government services. There was a missionary doctor, nurses and even a dentist. The hospital was well managed and had good supplies.

Over time, the government opened a hospital a few miles away and now the old hospital is only a health clinic, run by a national nurse. She is employed by the same mission agency and serves as any employed nurse would. Faith is not a part of the service and it is not connected to the church.

What did I learn from all this:

- Quality service was provided: physical, educational, and

spiritual. Those who were dignified enough to seek these got.

- Although the missionaries came from the same mission agency, there was not much connection between the various services.

- The services were institution-based with little community participation or involvement of local leaders.

- The missionaries seemed superior to the nationals as if they had it all. Most of us did not relate closely to them or what they were doing.

- They were experts in what they did. They were the ones who could do it well and so we looked up to them.

This background led me to make a choice. At age 13, I left my village and went to a boarding school in the city for High School. There I was exposed to missionaries from other denominations. When I graduated I decided I wanted to become a missionary but I wanted to do it differently than what I had seen growing up. I didn't want to stand out. I wanted to work with the poor and serve them at their level while involving them in the process and showing Christ to them. I did not have the whole formula together but I knew what I wanted to see.

Although I had grown up in a protestant church and gone to a school with a Protestant influence, I wanted to be a Catholic missionary. Their missionary style is what came closest to the picture I had in mind. They seemed to offer their lives totally, not just their services. They gave their commitment long term, not just so long as the family arrangements allowed. They took prayer and the practice of their faith seriously. Their allegiance seemed to be God focused.

When the Catholic nuns and priest I came across served, especially in hospitals or among the poor, they related closely, really connecting with the destitute and demonstrated love. I loved them and that was the model I wanted to emulate. But this path, I came to realize, is about being!

So, considering the move to a convent, I shared this with the significant people in my life. My pastor advised me I can be a Catholic missionary in practice but needed not become a catholic. My family, especially my big sister, strongly felt I needed to raise a family. It was very important. Festus setting the stage to propose assured me it would be more fulfilling if we went as a couple and even raised our children out there. All good counsel.

When it comes to transformation ministry, the nations need an example, a displayed model, something different, that they can emulate. Transformation brings about marked change that is irreversible. A seed, hatched out from its case, a shoot of hope 'with roots and leaves', a support system utilizing local resources, secure to grow. A caterpillar transformed into a butterfly with beauty, speed, productive activity, moving with ease, to reproduce.

The blue print is there. God created man in His image, and put him in a garden to tend it. We are called to partner with God to facilitate that.

The strategy for missions has shifted. There was a time when written messages would be delivered by runners, that improved some and we got to telegrams, now emails. In the same manner, there was a time when ministry operated in separate departments, development, medical, church planting. Medical care mainly focused on curative approaches. These were set up in institutions. Missionaries were coming to the field as long term career missionaries, sent by mission agencies from the west.

There was a time we could only do missions the conventional/ traditional style. That was just fine. It worked then and we knew no better. So we lived with the disadvantages of that strategy: creating dependency, killing dignity, lack of local ownership and limited to only what the vision bearer could handle. A person only has two hands.

This conventional way indeed has a history to overcome. It's a super power coming to a colony. The boss and the servant mentality. It comes with authority rather than love. If followed it will be seen as judgmental. The giver decides what the recipient needs, stages the show and leaves.

It's not easy to change, because it gives us service providers some advantages. It gives us ownership, limited to us and our direct efforts. We get to keep a job. We feel secure. We have a status, feel needed and we are the only ones with the skill. The credit is ours. We are heroes to the people we serve.

But the mission fields have changed. Indigenous mission agencies are springing up. National missionaries are going from one culture to another. Community based organizations are set up in big numbers and have made inroads in the communities. Churches have been planted. For the most part, even in closed countries, national Christians who speak languages of every people group as well as English can be identified, mobilized and facilitated to speed up the work. The advantage here is the cost effectiveness.

Technology has advanced and communication mediums are different. The gospel is made available in several innovative ways. Denomination lines are weakening and dying fast. A lot of new churches today are non denominational.

Again, there is the raised awareness that the problems we are dealing with like HIV/AIDS cut across departments and a wholistic approach is needed. These changes hit me coming back to Kenya after 7 years in Ethiopia.

It takes us back to Jesus' way of ministry: He made His disciples His co-workers in three years, becoming hands on participants. He delegated, with authority! He gave them authority to cast out demons! High profile skills in the hands of trainees.

Even with the knowledge that Peter will fail, He still tells him to feed His sheep. That would seem to border on carelessness. He even sends them out to do it alone. This allowed them to fail and learn from their shortcomings. Then, He hands it over! He actually phases out telling them, go therefore to the nations, after a pilot work in His local area, to do as He had taught them.

Jesus came to give His life. He thus multiplied himself in them. He did not come to give service, for that would have retained it to himself. His role was to demonstrate, train, empower, and step back to facilitate the establishment of His Father's kingdom on earth.

So what is this emerging ministry strategy? Based on my interaction with ministries in various countries in Central America, Asia, Middle east as well as in Africa, where by God's grace I have been involved in leadership training, I can boldly state that transformational strategies are the ones that are being favored by God. That is what He is blessing with lasting fruit.

On the other hand, God is actively spitting out what is not transformational. The grace for the former traditional approaches is gone. Time is running out and there is a sense of urgency in what God is doing. It is His show, His way, today.

What is coming up? Missionaries are changing from long term to short term teams. To go, make disciples, and phase out. The approaches are more integrated, church based and community based through partnerships: teams, rather than one person show.

The expatriate missionaries come to facilitate these partnerships, setting up foundations for well coordinated programs, that nationals as well as short term teams can plug into, with the nationals taking over as the expatriates shift gears. And these short term teams that are pouring into the mission fields are a great resource! I bear testimony to that, but only if they are utilized in these local partnership settings.

What are some cardinal signs of a transformational ministry?

- Training trainers: not directly giving services unless it is to demonstrate or make inroads.

- Church based partnerships at the church level.

- Empowering: giving only what they need, coming alongside what they have, taking them to the next level.

- Building dignity: Doing it <u>with</u> them not for them or to show them.

- Bringing deliverance: breaking the bondage through advocacy, education, skill development, economic empowerment, changed behavior, spiritual maturity.

- Planning a phase out strategy from the beginning.

- Marked by fruit after fruit rather than one time harvest– looking like fruit bearing trees rather than the seasonal plants.

- Self replenishing and not dependant on us or an external source or technology.

- Bathed in prayer, guided of God, for His glory.

- Giving of our lives not service.

How can we tell if we have empowered for transformation? It's in place when:

- We can take risks in delegating. For example, come to the point where we can say to our national partners - these are guests from my main supporting church. I will leave them with you for two days for you to show them our ministry.

- When we can take a year of furlough and do not need a replacement, and even if we are going back, we do not plan to go back to the same tasks.

- When to our surprise we realize that the local ministry has moved to the next level and has forgotten to inform us much less to consult us or ask permission.

- The systems for accountability are in nationals' hands and you are subject to those systems.

If after three to five years in the field we cannot comfortably have national teams run the show, we cannot relocate or take another role or open doors for others to partner, then we are failing.

It takes daily obedience. It is sometimes painful. I have been in the mission field for years and I am still taking baby steps in this. I am however determined to give my life rather than just service, whatever the packaging might be. I have learned that it is costly to give our lives to ministry. It is easier to give services and hold on to my life.

I am reminded of two occasions when I had to travel, once to Yemen and another time to Sudan. Both trips were from a mission field that was not my home country. At that time, Festus was away in seminary in the US. I left our two boys with a national worker in Ethiopia so that they could attend school. On both occasions I cried all the way to the airport. Then I was unable to return home as planned. On one of those occasions I was detained for being in a conflict zone. And, as though that was not enough, on both these occasions the boys were ill when I was away.

Soon, the next decision was made. The boys would go to boarding school. I remember the week before their departure and the first week after they were gone. I was not functional. It was like taking up the cross again to follow Christ, and even though broken hearted, releasing them so as to give my life. I want to quickly add, we cannot out give God. This year (2006) we are taking a furlough and we get to spend a year with our boys, now teenagers!

Death is a word that is not good news. It is a loss in the battle for life. Death is ugly, smells bad, the familiar is lost, shape is lost, what is of value is lost! It has a finality to it that is very uncomfortable. In death, we lose control, we are out of touch, even disconnected from self.

In John 12: 24, Jesus gave the example of a kernel of wheat saying unless it falls to the ground and dies, it remains only a single seed. But if it dies, it produces many seeds. No death means no fruit, at least not the kind that lasts.

Through death we are transformed, from one state of existence to another. The transformed, in partnership with God, can facilitate transformation. We come to the end of ourselves.

Sometimes our greatest spiritual transformations occur through pain. For the children of Israel, their forty years of wandering in the desert changed them as a people. Fasting for forty days and nights in the desert at the beginning of his ministry marked Jesus. Pain can foster some of our greatest moments of spiritual growth.

What specifically does this death do in our lives? It burns up bad spiritual fuel-our unhealthy motivation for wanting to serve in the first place. It is important to acknowledge that none of us did so out of a hundred percent pure, uninhibited love for God. We usually have ulterior motives. Some wanted to avoid hell, wanted to get fixed emotionally, wanted to please significant people in our lives. All of these factors play very heavily into ministry decisions. When difficult times arrive, we discover these motivations weren't nearly powerful enough to sustain dedication to Christ. The cost of remaining outweighs the original motivation for becoming one, so it comes to finding a new motivation or walking away.

When we live to see the results of our service, we eventually become dependent on these to sustain us. We begin to pursue the feelings we get from serving God rather than pursuing God Himself. When we come to a place where the feelings are taken away, we learn to love God for what He wants to do and not for what we can get from Him.

How can you tell you are becoming dead to self?

- When you hear someone telling what you did and the honor is credited to another and that is fine with you.

- When you look at the fields and realize the harvest being produced is beyond your direct capability or supervision, because several hands are participating and your name does not feature.

- When you no longer keep a list of what we have achieved.

But we still live if:

- We still retain our original identity, are doing the same tasks we went out to do and no disciples have taken over.

- The ministry is ours – it has our name written all over it and has yet to be passed on to anyone else.

- We are fearful to trust that someone else can handle things as well or better than we can.

There are days I realize I continue to die. On those days, part of me gets sad, because I realize I will never be the same again. It makes it difficult for those who knew the former me to understand or relate to me. But I also realized that I have been totally set free to follow Christ.

We were sorting out stuff recently to relocate, yet again. Stuff from twelve years ago when we left home was still in storage boxes. Three piles came up. Give away, sell, and carry. Notice throw away is not a category in the mission field. Everything can innovatively be put to use. That carry pile keeps on changing and has been much reduced.

Anyway, as we sorted our worldly possessions, I came across the first English Bible I ever owned—the Revised Standard Version. Written on the back cover were the words: "There was a day Florence (Ndinda Mbevi) Muindi died to..." and went on to list the dear things a high school girl would choose to relinquish.

There was a time I died to having a home. Tied that to a balloon and let it go. We have had houses to stay in and enjoyed living in them, but so far, no home. If God gives us one, we know it will not be hard to even then, give it up.

You think you are dead until you get to a new level in life, for example, a fresh spiritual gift, a promotion, a new phase in life, and it is time to die again. And some of those things you die to are very capable of resurrecting. Dying daily becomes an ongoing life style, for those of us who want to give our lives, not service.

This message could end as mere information sharing. But I know that it is an example of the kind of ministry Jesus came for and left for us to follow. And He will cause it to come about. This is the 'agenda on the wall' in the first decade of this millennium.

When Isaiah announced Jesus' mission in Isaiah 61:11, he concluded by saying: *For as soil makes a sprout come up, and a garden causes seeds to grow, so the sovereign LORD will make righteousness and praise spring up before the nations.*

As Jesus left, He told us who are his disciples in Matt 28:19 to go and make disciples of all nations, baptizing them, and teaching them to obey everything. It is by teaching, by example, by the giving of our lives in love. To that end, He promises to be with us.

It's an all or nothing law. If we do not take up the cross totally – we cannot be His disciples and therefore cannot make disciples. He gives the terms — to deny of ourselves and take the death prescription so we can bring forth fruit of eternal value.

Appendix

Life in Abundance Today

"Africa is beyond bemoaning the past for its problems. The task of undoing that past is on the shoulders of African leaders themselves, with the support of those willing to join in a continental renewal. We have a new generation of leaders who know that Africa must take responsibility for its own destiny, that Africa will uplift itself only by its own efforts in partnership with those who wish her well."

— *Nelson Mandela*

Dr. Muindi's story is compelling and humbling especially for those of us fortunate enough to work day in and day out with her. As an organization, Life in Abundance International now has over seventy employees who work in two continents and in eight countries. These staff members are the quintessential essence of what Mr. Mandela refers to as the 'new generation of leaders' who strive tirelessly to turn the tide of poverty that perpetually challenges the African spirit.

Hundreds of communities have been impacted. Thousands of individuals have been trained to become trainers, passing on information and skills to others. Thousands of families have broken the cycle of dependency and poverty, launching out in income generating activities with new found faith, healed emotions, and affirmed dignity. Thousands of orphaned and vulnerable children have been reached. Close to a million individuals have received help through community mobilizing activities exemplified by health education campaigns and medical camps. The changed lives, of those impacted by others tell the story.

In Ethiopia, over one thousand orphans and vulnerable children, some totally living on the streets, have been effectively reached and rehabilitated. The response to AIDs through health education, church based care and support groups, youth programs, prevention of transmission from mother to child, as well as testing and counseling, has had its impact. The hope that is generated and visible keeps us serving.

As a visionary and leader, Dr. Muindi has assembled a team of national leaders who are both the hope of the world and the hope of the poor in the communities where we work. These national leaders are not our collective hope because of what they will do singlehandedly. Rather, they choose to serve in such a way that they empower local pastors and lay leaders to restore their communities to God, and to one another. LIA is not expressly a leadership development organization, but the heart and practical output of our ministry is spreading the vision that God gave Dr. Muindi many years ago: to transform communities by mobilizing, training, and empowering churches to implement wholistic ministries focusing on the poor.

We believe that in Christ, the local Church was designed to wholisti-cally meet the needs of their community. In the areas where we work, our church partners are able realize this vision after they have been equipped and empowered to do so. In turn, they will equip and em-power their lay leaders in such a way that the wholistic ministry will be multiplied and expanded. This is LIA at its best: a new generation of faithful African leaders inspiring local pastors and lay leaders 'to be Jesus' in their community.

As Mr. Mandela states, this work cannot be undertaken without partners who wish Africa well. Thank you for joining Dr. Muindi and LIA in wholistically transforming the lives of marginalized and impoverished individuals.

Further information on LIA or support for this ministry can be facilitated by visiting the website: www.liaint.org

Justin Narducci
LIA USA Director

Acronyms

AMREF   African Medical and Research Foundation

CHE   Community Health Evangelism

CMF   Christian Missionary Fellowship

GTZ   Germany Technical Aid Organization

LIA   Life in Abundance International

PA   The State of Pennsylvania

UN   United Nations

UNFPA   United Nations Family Planning Association

UNICEF   United Nations Children Fund

US/USA   United States of America

VBS   Vacation Bible School

For further information about the ministry of Life in Abundance International or to contact the author, you can write to:

Life in Abundance International
1605 East Elizabeth St. Ste U-7B
Pasadena, CA 91104
USA

T 626 213 2203
F 866 LIA 3336
Email: admin@liaint.org

* The use of the word 'wholistic ministry' is the preference of the author.